yes, ma'am

KATE-LYNN ELIZABETH
S.L. FORRESTER

Copyright © 2023 S.L.Forrester and Kate-Lynn Elizabeth

Yes Ma'am by S.L.Forrester and Kate-Lynn Elizabeth

All rights reserved. This book or any portion thereof may not be reproduced or used in any manner whatsoever without the express written permission of the publisher except for the use of brief quotations in a book review, or as permitted by U.S copyright law.

Independently published.

Please continue to support independent authors by obtaining their work from reputable sources, including online and physical bookstores. Let's work together in reducing the harm done to authors and readers by avoiding piracy and unofficial copies of authors' works.

This is a work of fiction. Names, characters, places, and incidents either are the product of the author's imagination or are used factiously. Any resemblance to actual persons, living or dead, businesses, companies, events, or locals is entirely coincidental.

Cover designer: CPR Designs

First edition

Contents

Dedication	V
Prologue	1
Izzy	14
1. Chapter 1	15
Izzy	26
2. Chapter 2	27
Izzy	40
3. Chapter 3	41
Izzy	52
4. Chapter 4	53
Izzy	70
5. Chapter 5	71
Izzy	90
6. Chapter 6	91
Izzy	106
7. Chapter 7	107

Izzy	120
8. Chapter 8	121
Izzy	144
9. Chapter 9	145
Izzy	156
10. Chapter 10	157
Izzy	166
11. Chapter 11	167
Izzy	178
12. Chapter 12	179
Acknowledgments	192
About Authors	196
Also By S.L.Forrester	197

Dedicated to everybody that struggles with life. Remember:
ONE DAY AT A TIME.

TRIGGER WARNINGS

Drug addiction

Loosely BDSM

Unexpected Pregnancy with a side character

Gun Violence

Kidnapping

Death of a side character

Mention of Drug Support Group

Breath Play

Prologue

July 12

Thirty-five...

Another year around the sun. Another year of doing my own thing, watching my best friend and his girlfriend, – sorry fiancée. Jace proposed in a bar a couple of weeks ago.

Makes me almost want to settle down and do the same thing they are.

Building a life together.

Growing old with the same person, every day.

Loving and choosing the same person. Every. Day.

Almost.

I sit outside, in their new backyard on the brand new deck, drinking a vodka tonic.

"So..." Jace clears his throat from behind me. I crane my neck back, so I can look at him. I watch him stride from the back door to where he is now standing beside me.

"So... What?" I laugh.

"How's it feel being thirty-five?" he chuckles.

"Uhh, what kind of question is that? You're older than me. I should be asking you that question, not the other way around." I roll my eyes at him and turn back to look out over their backyard.

They picked the perfect place to build a family home. Not too far out of town to be an inconvenience, but also not in town to have prying eyes looking over their fence to get a peek at what is going on, on the daily. It is really peaceful out here and it makes me just a little jealous of what they have going for them. I push the thought to the back of my mind as Jace starts talking again.

He takes a seat in the Adirondack chair next to me, losing a sigh as he settles in. "Just because I'm older doesn't mean shit. How are you doing? I know the whole thing with Elise has been hard on you and –" I cut him off.

"Nope. No. Stop right now. We are not talking about that. This is supposed to be a happy day. Remember? It's my birthday. Don't make the birthday girl sad. I chose to be here with you guys instead of getting my pussy licked." With that, I raise my drink to the sky and make a silent toast to help me get through the rest of this day if I am to be fielding questions like these. I take a long gulp and wait for him to reply.

"What do you mean we aren't talking about it?" Jace asks.

"Exactly what I fucking said, dumbass. We. Are. Not. Talking. About. It." I make sure I enunciate each word just in case he didn't hear me the first time.

"Fine, but you can't run from this forever. We will talk." I glance over and catch him giving me the side eye while taking a pull from his beer. I grumble under my breath, not looking forward to that day. The worst part of it is, we work together. I can't hide from him for very long...

And with that, Ash comes to my rescue before he can try talking about this shit again.

"Jace! Izzy! Get your asses in here! It's time for cake!" she calls from the patio doors, waving us in. "Don't make me come out there and drag you both in. Let's. Go!" I'm shocked at the volume she gets from only a couple of feet away and I look at Jace.

"She okay?" I ask.

Jace nods and gets up from his chair. "She's been stressed lately at the shop. There have been some guys coming in almost every day, just to call her coffee shit."

"Can't she call the cops on them or something for trespassing?" We walk to the back door slowly and Jace finally answers as he reaches for the handle to open the door for me to go through.

Pausing before moving again, he starts and gives a sigh, "She's tried. She refused their service and asked them to leave but when she called the cops they didn't do anything for her. She did everything she was supposed to, but they are on public property so it's a weird thing to get into. Cops all have different opinions, it doesn't matter if it is trespassing or not... if the cop won't remove them, she can't do anything about it. So she just ignores them, poor Clara though because she's the one that gets most of the complaints from other customers..." I want to go over there and kick their asses. Actually, I think I will. Jace leans in and says, "Please don't tell her I told you. She doesn't want anyone to know that this is getting to her."

I nod my head. "Scouts honor." I raise my left hand, holding up three fingers.

"I think that only applies if you were a Scout." Jace laughs, shaking his head. "Get in there birthday girl, you need to have the first slice." With that, he opens the door and jerks his head towards the entrance, motioning me to step inside. It's weird but I go anyways.

"Why are the lights–" I start to ask but just as I do the lights come on and...

"HAPPY BIRTHDAY!!" I jump and back up a few steps, crashing into Jace, who followed me inside. I scream and turn around to face him.

"You said there wasn't going to be a big party!" I yell, punching him in the gut.

He bends over, holding his stomach. "Did I?" He stands and grabs his chin with his thumb and forefinger, looking to the ceiling, thinking. "Must have slipped my mind then." He smiles. I whirl around and march toward Ash, the brains of the operation.

"What did you do?!" I scold.

"What did I do? What did *I* do? You–" I cut Ash off as her volume starts to increase and I lay my hands on her shoulders, pushing her back into the kitchen where we have more privacy.

"You know I didn't want a big party for my birthday. I am only thirty-five. That is nothing to celebrate…"

"That is exactly why I did it. You're *thirty-five*! Any age is worth celebrating!" The anger I thought I had picked up on earlier is completely gone now. Leaving no trace of it behind.

"Alright, well it better not last long. I have to open the gym tomorrow at five. Plus, I want to find somebody to stick my finger in," I say.

"Don't worry, I told everyone that they have to be gone by six," Ash giggles, pushing me back out to where everyone is. "Let's do cake!" she shouts from behind me.

Everyone crowds around and I cringe at the offkey singing of the traditional tune. By the end I have blown out the numbered candles, showing off my correct age. *Thanks, Jace…* I have the honor, according to Ash, to cut the first slice of this massive cake. There is no way we will be able to eat all of this today.

The cake is my favorite red velvet, spanning 2 tiers and covered in frosting. It looks heavenly and I resist the urge to take the biggest piece for myself. Turning back to the crowd I start passing out servings to the rest of the guests at their request for sizes, as this cake is way too big.

I talk with a few of my coworkers and our conversation mostly gravitates around the work variety. We aren't the type of people to socialize outside of work that isn't at a bar and drunk after some awful people have come through during operating hours. After a while, I manage to make it all the way around the room and talk with everybody.

Everyone from the gym and Ash's coffee shop is here. It's only Clara; they haven't hired anyone else yet but they are doing interviews in the coming weeks. I catch Silas in the back corner of the room next to some girl I don't recognize. I smile, knowing Ash is probably freaking out that her son has a girlfriend at roughly the same age she was when he was born. I need to remember to get some condoms to slip him.

Coming to the far side of the room, I notice a long table of pretty boxes with bows on it. I never expected any of this. Tears threaten to spring up and I have to excuse myself to the bathroom before I end up causing a scene, over unexpected gifts no less. It was never a requirement to attend but some still did.

Emerging from the bathroom a few minutes later, I scan the room, searching for the familiar head of dark hair and where he went. Spotting him, I make my way through the crowd of people, thanking everyone for coming as I go.

"You knew and let me walk in here without telling me. Asshole." I shove into his shoulder, getting his attention.

"Yeah I did, and I would do it again. You suck at keeping secrets," Jace says.

"I do not! I kept that picture for your housewarming a secret for over a year! You both had no idea I even had it!" I exclaim.

"True, but when it comes to something you don't want to do. You suck at pretending to be surprised," he chuckles.

I cross my arms and pretend to pout. "Do not." And I stick my tongue out at him.

"Happy birthday by the way. I know I said it outside but it's a party now and needs to be said again." I smile and thank him again.

The party continues for a few hours. I thank each person as they leave, telling my coworkers I'll see them at work in the morning. Turning back to the room, I look at Ash, Jace, and Silas.

"Never throw me a surprise party again." I deadpan.

Ash starts to tear up. "You didn't like the party?" a whimper escapes her lips.

"I didn't say that. I said to never throw me a *surprise* party again. Do the party all you want. Just let me know when it is happening. Please. Also, next time invite some hot chicks," I clarify. Ash sniffs and wipes a stray tear rolling down her cheek.

"So you liked it? Right?" she asks.

"Yes, Ash. I liked the party. It was actually pretty fun," I agreed. Looking around the room, I see the aftermath of what happened in the last couple of hours. "Do you need me to help clean up? I don't need to leave for another couple of hours, so I can help." I offer.

"No! You're the birthday girl, you don't have to lift a finger." Ash argues.

"Ash. Come on, look around. This is going to take you guys hours to clean. There is gift wrap, dishes, and just stray shit everywhere. Why not take the help?" I push.

"Iz, I wouldn't push it any further. Let's just go to the basement and let Ash do what she needs to. She won't even let me do the dishes anymore, so I surrender the fact she needs to do it her way. Let's go." Jace waves me to follow behind him and we head to the basement. Before heading down the stairs, I look up and call Ash.

"If you need *any* help, please call for it!" And continue down the stairs.

"I won't! Have fun!" Ash calls back as I'm halfway down.

Walking into the recreational room in their basement, they have a huge T.V. along the one wall, a large L-shaped sofa on the opposite wall, and a coffee table in the middle over a large fluffy rug that I guarantee Ash picked out. Jace is standing in front of the T.V. turning it on and setting up a streaming service.

"What do you want to watch? She won't stop until it's done tonight. So we got time to watch, whatever," Jace says without turning around.

"Doesn't matter to me, you pick." I look around the room, searching for Silas. He came down with us but he is nowhere to be found now. "Where did Silas go?" I ask.

"Probably to his room, it's just over there." Jace points down a hall at the other end of the large room. "He wanted to have his own space, 'far away from the noise'." He uses air quotes around the last part and I can't help but laugh.

"Hears you guys too much, huh?" I asked.

"What gave you that idea?" he chuckles and looks back to the T.V. "But seriously, what do you want to watch?"

All emotion drains from my face and I stare directly at him. "Porn." He rolls his eyes. "I told you, you pick. I don't care what we watch. Just pick something." I move to flop down in the corner of the L and stretch out with my legs, taking up most of the short end. Sinking into the couch, I sigh and Jace sits in the middle, still scrolling through the choices. "Jace..." I groan.

"What? Ash picks what we watch recently..." He admits.

"Well then, what haven't you gotten to watch that you miss? At this point, I'll fall asleep right here before you pick something," I joke.

"Fine," he says. We end up watching *Friends* for about an hour and a half before I decide it is time for me to head back home so I can sleep before work in the morning. I didn't realize how fast Ash moves when she wants to.

When we get back upstairs into the living room, it looks like there was never even a party here. All the wrapping and dishes have been removed and nothing looks out of place. Ash doesn't even look phased or worn out when we finally find her in the kitchen, doing the dishes.

"Hey," I say calmly, coming up behind Ash to let her know I was there. "I'm going to head out. I gotta get to bed before I become a grouch in the morning. Jace can attest to that." With that, I look over my shoulder to see Jace nodding his head.

"Awe, I wanted to hang out with you a little before you had to go. I was almost done, but it's okay. I understand you need your sleep. I put all your gifts in your trunk by the way, so don't worry about those." *I totally forgot about the gifts...* "Go. We will hang out this weekend. Promise?" Ash wipes her hands on her jeans and turns to face me while she talks. I nod. She reaches out, pulls me in for a hug, and walks me to the front door with Jace. I say bye to them, hugging both again, and ask them to tell Silas I said goodbye. Promising they would, they close the door behind me as I walk out.

Finally sitting in my car and being alone, feels like the best thing in the world. I slump back into my captain's seat and take a few breaths. Jace and Ash seem so happy together. I don't need to settle down, do I?

No, fuck that! I shake the thought from my head and think to myself. I am still young, thirty-five isn't that old! I don't even want kids, so there is no issue in being 'too old' to settle down. I can still party with the best of them, and that is exactly what I plan on doing.

It takes about twenty minutes to drive back to my apartment. I unlock the front door, step in, and set my bag and keys on the little table I refurbished and painted from a thrift store in the next town over. Dragging myself to the bathroom, stripping clothes off as I go. I turn on the shower and let it get hot.

Looking at myself in the full-length mirror. I inspect my body - pasty skin, toned stomach, a little more than a handful of tits, blonde hair that comes past my breasts, clean shaved kitty, and mile-long legs. Smiling, I turn and step under the scalding water. I stand there for a few minutes before starting my routine, letting the water run over my body and relaxing my muscles.

As I lather up my curves with my loofa, my mind wanders to my last one-night stand. She liked to be tossed around, and liked to get her platinum hair pulled. Damn, she was fun. Thinking about it has me pushing my thighs together.

I usually don't touch myself but I can't resist this time. I massage my boobs, pinch my nipples and run my hand down my stomach, stopping right above my clit. I separate my middle and pointer fingers to make an upside-down V, and pinch my clit enough to give me the stinging pain. I lean back on the tiles and lift my leg up to rest my foot on the edge of the shower.

One hand pinches my nipple and the palm of the other hand rubs my clit while I dip my fingers into my entrance. I look down at myself and watch the water run down my boobs, over my belly button and form a puddle between my pussy and hand. The warm feeling starts to build and my leg starts to shake, my head falls back and I bite my bottom lip. When my climax hits, it's not great but it will get me by for the night.

I step out of the shower after the orgasm I just gave myself, not the same as with another girl but will do for now. I dry myself off, throw my hair up into a messy bun and crash down onto the couch in my small living room with a bowl of stale popcorn I made last night. I turn on the T.V. and search through the options to stream. I land on *Supernatural* and press play.

"Happy birthday to me," I sigh.

Chapter 1

Two months later

Something is on my leg and there's an arm lying over my stomach.

Shit.

I open my eyes and have to close them immediately. It's too bright. I take a minute to remember where I am—a hotel room. The walls are stained yellow with cigarette smoke and the carpet is a puke-green color.

Last night was crazy. I got so fucked up, I don't remember leaving the club and I definitely don't remember the two girls in bed with me. I look down and find the weight I felt on my leg is one of the girls' legs. The girl lying over my stomach has the blanket wrapped around her and the other is butt-ass naked with no shame. She's on her back and her boobs are on full display.

Usually, I would stick around to play a little more but I actually have plans today and Ash would be pissed if I didn't show up. She has finally decided to settle down with my dipshit best friend and I asked to take her dress shopping. What I really want to do is help her find the perfect lingerie to wear under it. Jace doesn't talk to me about their sex life because he wants to be respectful but Ash... she can't stop talking about it.

You would think being a parent would get in the way but that's not slowing her down at all. Bringing myself back to what's in front of me, I run a hand over my face and brace myself for what I am about to do. Gently, I slip out my pinned arm and try to free my leg. I take it slow, waking them up would be a disaster. I told them like I tell everybody else, *'I only want a good time and only for one night. I don't do relationships'*.

The thing about me is that I have to be in control when it comes to sex. Well, when it comes to most things. It's hard to find women that will be up for it. I tried it with one before but only one person can't fill my needs.

I get out of bed without disturbing anybody and slip back into my white lace panties and black skinny jeans. I see my white shirt on the floor across the room but can't find my bra. *It has to be here somewhere.* It's my favorite one.

I search under the bed, the hallway, and the bathroom. Shit, I don't see it. Whatever, I have to get going. I pull my shirt over my head, and grab my socks and shoes but decided to just carry them.

I get my wallet, keys, and phone that miraculously ended up together on a side table by the door, and sneak out. I look for my car but it's not in the parking lot. I was drunk, so that makes sense. *Fuck.* Now I have to wait for an uber, Ash is going to murder me. I call for a ride and get lucky because they are only three minutes away.

Might as well bite the bullet and text her.

> **ME: dont kill me**
>
> **ASH: Where the hell are you?**
>
> **ME: im waiting on the uber. be there soon**
>
> **ASH: This was your fucking idea! Get here!**
>
> **ME: lets take a breath**
>
> **ASH: Let's learn how to text. Did you know that your phone has capital letters and punctuation?**
>
> **ME: DID YOU FORGET YOUR BITCH PILL TODAY????**
>
> **ME: oh look... i found the buttons**

My ride pulls up but I'm not stupid enough to tell the driver my name or just hop in. I motion for him to roll the window down.

"Sup, who are you here for?" I ask him. He looks to be a million years old. Almost all the way bald with a small patch of gray right below his neck. The glasses that are resting on the tip of his nose are so thick that I am now scared for my life from his driving. He obviously can't fucking see. How is he driving?

"Miss Izzy," he responds with one of those old people's smiles. It's sweet but creepy at the same time. I smile and get in the back seat.

"Take me to the Bridal Shop on 4th Avenue, please," I say in the sweetest voice that I can muster up.

> **ME: im in a car now. ill see you in ten minutes if i dont die**

> **ASH: I will be so pissed if you die. Who else will tell me if I look like shit?**

> **ME: i dont know how jace got so lucky with you**

She has been uncharacteristically bitchy lately. Apparently, wedding planning isn't fun for her like it is for every other female in the world. I don't understand how she is stressed though. Jace proposed a week after they moved into the house they built together and has been planning it ever since.

That was a year ago. Her attitude started a couple of months ago but they haven't set a date or anything. I'm at a loss with her lately. When I'm around her, I stay in my lane and do as I'm told.

We pull up to the place and I pay the driver that's going to croak over any minute now. I grab my stuff, get out and walk through the single door. My socks are stuffed into my shoes, which I am still carrying. An uptight woman who has her blonde hair in the tightest bun and red lipstick that is not her shade and doesn't look good walks up to me and stares at my feet.

"Ma'am, you need to put those shoes on when you are in here," she says shortly.

"Will do. Thanks. Oh, and can I get one of those fancy glasses of champagne?" I walk away before she answers. Ash is standing in front of three mirrors that show her front and both sides. The dress that she's wearing is a tight ariel with laces woven up the back keeping it on. The laces are loose enough to show off some skin that starts right above her ass and goes all the way to her upper back. It has thin spaghetti straps and it's more off-white.

"You look beautiful." It's the truth. She doesn't have a body that looks like she grew a person in it.

"Well of course you would say that. What kind of person would you be if you said I looked like shit? You would be a fucked up person, that's what," she bites my head off but then shakes her head as she looks to the floor.

"Thank you. I don't know about this one though. I think I want something a little loose, ya know." She smooths down her stomach with her hands, turning from side to side.

"Looser? I thought you liked showing off your curves?" I look at her with confusion. She turns to look at me with a serious face. What am I missing?

"My curves? Do you think I have big hips or something? What is it, my ass is too huge for you?" Ash has always had a mouth on her but this is crazy. "Jace hasn't spoken to you about me? Has he?" she whispers and looks down at the floor in front of her.

"About what?" She has to tell me now. She looks so serious.

"Yeah, so, uhh..." she begins, still looking down. This is making me nervous. What can she possibly have to tell me? "he knocked me up. I mean not on purpose! He's not that fucking stupid, I switched from the pill to the implant. I knew that the chances of getting pregnant were high the first month after the switch but we always wrap it up. They weren't expired or anything, I don't know what happened but they did and here we are. Old and pregnant." Her eyes finally meet mine when she doesn't hear a response and I take a step back, trying to hold in my laughter. I can't hold it in any longer and start at a small giggle because she was so against having more. Silas is her only kid and he just turned 17. It's so funny to me; she doesn't think so and her expression is telling me to shut the fuck up. But I can't. I laugh so hard and so loud that the lady from earlier looks over our way.

"Well, congrats! As soon as you get one almost out the door, you welcome another in." I try to rein it in but damn, her face makes it even more hilarious. But then she looks at me with glassy eyes. Oh no, no no no no. I don't do crying, I can't. "Hey now, stop that. I was just playing around. I am happy for you both and I'm going to be the best damn aunt the world has ever seen. So cut that shit out." I can feel myself starting to panic when her tears start falling. Shit. The lady walks over, watching Ash.

"Oh sweetheart, you look beautiful. This one is perfect," she gushes, assuming it's happy tears. Oh, how wrong she is. I pull my phone out of my pocket and text Jace.

> ME: i broke her. What do i do

> JACE: What did you do?

> ME: i laughed when she told me about the baby

> **JACE: Damnit Iz! She has had a shit time processing this already.**

> **ME: well if you told me in the first place then we wouldn't be here. How do i fix her**

> **JACE: Tell her how cute she is. I'm on the way.**

Tell her how cute she is... That I can do. I hope it works.

"Damn, Ash. Your ass looks so good in that dress," I tell her. "I'm jealous as hell that Jace gets to bite that thing. Lucky bastard." I'm trying but she isn't falling for it. She stares at me like I'm fucking stupid. At this point, I feel it. The lady that has something stuck up her ass has a dumb look on her face.

I was going to tell her Jace is on his way but I know she will flip out on me for texting him, so I will let that be a surprise. Speak of the devil and he shall appear. The door opens and a very concerned man walks in. Jace is wearing light blue jeans with a gray button-up and black sneakers.

I quickly put my socks and shoes on and slip out the door. I don't want to sit and be blamed for something when I can leave and go home. I call another uber to come to get me and take me to the bar so I can get my car. I just want a hot shower right now, the rest of my day can wait.

When the car pulls up, it's the same old guy from the first time.

"It looks like we are the best of friends now," he laughs and I swear it looks like his dentures are about to pop out. I get in, tell him where to take me, and start playing on my phone.

My apartment is pretty basic. One bathroom and one bedroom, a small kitchen with hardly any cabinet space, and an old ass stove. The living room counts as a dining room and I have my drawings hung up all over. I've always had a thing for art, I don't know what it is but I'm attracted to it. It's my outlet.

I'm on the third floor and there is a family that lives above me. It's very fucking annoying having to hear the kids stomping around at all hours of the day and night. Sometimes just for shits and giggles, I started moaning really loud even though nothing is going on.

I tell their mom when I see her in the mailroom to shut them up but she always tells me to fuck off and go whore around somewhere else. She's a bitch that obviously hasn't had an orgasm in a long time. Normally I would help out on that but no amount of alcohol will get me to go through her jungle. It might even fucking bite.

I walk to my bedroom, put my phone on the charger, and go to my bathroom to turn the shower on. This morning has been one big shitshow. I can't believe my best friend is going to have a baby. Jace always wanted one but since Ash said never again, he was more than happy to step up and be the male parent to Ash's son, Silas, he was missing in his life through Layne, his biological father.

The deadbeat... I remember Jace telling me how hellbent she was on not having any more kids. Guess that didn't work out for her. They are kind of old to start over, with Jace being 37 and Ash 32. Ok, so, hers isn't bad but he is getting too old for that shit. I love babies and they will probably get tired of me being over there when that kid pops out.

My shower heats up so I take my clothes off and step in. The hot water feels amazing running down my body. There's a slight sting on my hip and I look down. That bitch bit me last night.

If I see her again, that ass is going to be bright red. They all know the rules: *don't leave marks*. I can't stand it when they try my patience. It's done and over with now so I move on and wash my hair and body.

Reluctantly, I get out and dry off. Throwing on black leggings and a white tank top, I think about my next move. I cleared my day so that I could spend it helping with dress shopping but since that went downhill, I'm going to sit on my couch with popcorn and binge-watch *The Vampire Diaries* for the twelfth time. I'm just tired and I don't really want to go out to parties every night anymore.

It was fun in my twenties but I'm 35 and that's too old to be fucking around. Maybe it's time to stop fucking everything with a vagina and start looking for an actual person with a brain. Being with one person for the rest of my life doesn't sound that great though.

Damnit.

Chapter 2

Work is a bitch this morning. It's just a bunch of meatheads. Ms. Beth twisted her ankle earlier this year so Jace had to start working with some guy. The man-kid has zero muscles, the wind could probably break him.

"Excuse me, ma'am." There's a girl about my height standing in front of the counter. She has short, wavy, brown hair, chocolate eyes, and is thick like a goddess. She's wearing purple leggings and a black, loose shirt. Damn, she would look good kneeling in front of me...waiting for a command.

"What can I do for you, Mrs...?" I don't see a ring but that doesn't mean anything. There are a lot of people that don't wear jewelry to work out.

"Miss, actually. My name is Hasley. I was wondering if there's anybody that could help me. I've never been here before and I have no idea what I'm doing." She gives me her name and I bet it will roll off of my tongue like honey later tonight.

"So you need a personal trainer?" I ask even though my job is behind the desk, I will go out there just to have my hands on her.

"I didn't know that was an option. I absolutely need that." Her eyes light up and I'm going to take it. I look her up and down one more time to get that body embroidered in my brain. Even if I don't go home with her tonight, I'll still take care of myself later.

"Let's get you set up with a membership. And don't worry about the fees, it's on me." I will do whatever I have to to get her to come around more. I give her my smoothest smile but she looks to the side like she's offended. I have so many things to say to her but it will just scare her off. One step at a time. Let's get her set up and then later I will pounce.

"I can afford it, I don't need you to take care of the money," she's snappy. I'm going to have to fix that. I just smile and continue writing her up. She tells me her address, gives me her card for payment…which I don't input…and tells me what she's trying to work on.

"You want to slim down?" I ask because there's no way I heard that right.

"Yeah, I mean, look at me. I haven't been on a date in years because as soon as they see me, they leave." She blows my mind with that. I want to tell her what I would do to that fucking body of hers but I can't…yet.

"Do you prefer a guy or girl…as a trainer?" I hold my breath, waiting for her answer. *Please want a girl, please want a girl.*

"A female, please. I don't want a man to have his hands on me right now," she says.

"No problem." I can't look away from her. Those pale lips, thick and juicy. I wonder what it would taste like sucked between my teeth. I take my time dragging my eyes up to hers. "Here's your membership card. We have a locker room with showers and a steam room. You don't need to wear anything under your towel when you go in. It helps with the whole process," I tell her. Oh, the images running through my mind right now. Her naked, laying on the bench with those beautiful breasts on full display… just for me. Fuck, between my thighs are wet.

She takes the card and watches me as I try to get my mind off of the naughty things running through it.

"Ok, so I will give you a tour of the place and we can talk about where you are physically and what you want to work on." No part of that is my job but I will take what I can get.

After I show her the workout area, the locker room, showers, and the sauna, I look into her eyes. She seems overwhelmed with everything and I wish I could kiss the stress lines between her eyebrows.

"Now, what are your goals?" I ask her.

"You're going to train me?" Confusion is all over her face. I slowly drag my eyes from her ankles to her eyes.

"I'm all yours." I let that drip from my mouth, in so many ways I mean it. A pink blush kisses her cheeks. There we go, some kind of reaction to me. She clears her throat and stretches her arms out, away from her hips.

"I want to lose this," she gestures to her stomach and sides and I can't help but get pissed off. I walk closer to her. Our shoes almost touch.

"Say one more bad thing about your body and I will make your tongue work harder than it ever has before," I threaten her. "Now, let's start with walking on the treadmill, get your heart pumping." I turn and walk over to them, not checking to see if she is following. Her body is fucking perfect and she will learn. I stop when I get to an empty one and wait for her to step on.

"Start slow and work yourself up to a speed walk. I'll be back in thirty minutes. Do you have a water bottle?"

"No, I forgot," she says and looks at me like she can't believe I would even ask. Of course I want to fuck the girl that doesn't give a shit about her health. I don't respond. I leave her and get one of the empty bottles that we sell. I fill it up with cool water and take it to her.

"Here, this is yours. Drink," I command.

"Thanks for your concern but I already have a mom, I don't need another," she bites back. I keep how much I like the idea of her calling me 'mommy' to myself.

"Oh, sweetheart, if you only knew." I take a step back before I do something that will make her leave. "I'll get you a hand towel for you to wipe your head."

Heading over to get her a towel I think about how nice she would taste on my tongue. Fuck, the feeling of my pants rubbing that spot begging for attention. I don't remember the last time somebody actually knew what they were doing down there. I enjoy being on my knees for them anyways but it would be nice to actually get off every once in a while.

Ash keeps telling me to start a vibrator collection but I would rather wait for a female's touch. Plus, it helps the practice of self-control.

I snag a towel and go back to my sweaty goddess. She may not know it yet but I will have my fingers inside of her tonight. When I get back to her, she's running.

"That's kinda like walking if you don't think about it," I tell her. She slows down to a walk and rolls her eyes.

"I want to lose the fat. Walking isn't going to make that happen," she responds with the wrong words. I tried to keep my needs in check but she has pushed it. I turn the treadmill off and walk over to the pull-up bar. I can hear the hardness of her breath behind me. Good, I'm glad her head isn't completely empty.

"Can I have the towel?" she asks. I don't say anything until we get there. I stop, turn to face her, and just stand there. Why does she talk down about herself? She's fucking perfect.

"Please." It's a statement. Manners are a big deal to me. It's what separates the assholes from the civilized. She looks at me confused. "You want something from me, right? I didn't hear the word 'please' come out of those sexy full lips. Try again," I tell her with a straight face. This catches her off guard and she can't seem to form words. The pink in her cheeks lets me know that she's embarrassed but likes it at the same time.

"Please," she says simply. I give her a small smile and take a step closer. She is maybe an inch shorter than me and her smell is intoxicating—strawberries with a hint of musk. Without a word, I fold the towel up a couple of times and lightly wipe her brow. I hear her breath catch and that just encourages me.

"I'm not into girls," she tells me but her body says otherwise.

"Oh, my sweet pet. A noodle is always straight until you get it wet." That darkens her flush. She squeezes her thighs together and that heats the flame inside me. I watch her bite her lip and I lick mine. Damn. "Hold on to the bar and start the pull-ups." She doesn't respond but moves to do as she's told. I feel eyes on me so I turn my head to figure out who it is. Jace. He has a smirk smacked on his face and he looks down, shaking his head. Fucker better keep his distance and not mess this up.

I bring my attention back to Hasley and notice her struggling. I am about to tell her to stop and take a break but a better plan comes to mind. I step up behind her and jump up to grab the same bar on either side of her hands. I wrap my legs around her hips and help pull her up.

The touch alone almost sends me over. She's warm and feels so good between my legs. Every time we pull up, she grunts. But it doesn't sound like a straining noise. It's more of a moan. She likes this, wants it.

I keep myself together for another four and once my feet hit the floor I take several steps back. There needs to be distance. I want to lick the sweat off of her neck. Run my tongue over her nipples that I can clearly see through her shirt.

"I can't do any more with you today. Jace can help you with the rest," I tell her and point to Jace. Her face drops but only for a second. I almost miss it but it was there. She straightens and a nervous look takes over but she tries to hide it.

"I've never had a girl hit on me before but it seems to be the same as a guy. All the talking just leads to disappointment. I don't need your friend over there, I know how to get things done myself," she says and I can feel my eyes pop out of my head. I close them for a moment to compose myself. She really fucked up.

I want to grab her wrist and pull her to the shower. I want to get those fucking clothes off of her. I want to drop to my knees and shove my tongue as deep into her pussy as I can get. I want to do those things but that isn't happening.

She's never been fucked by a woman before and when I get my hands on her, the entire building will hear her screams. When I open my eyes, she is shaking. Her nerves are apparent.

"Tell me what you want," I ask her as I slowly walk closer. Her brows come together in confusion. I get close enough to where I can whisper. "Tell me what you are needing at this moment, pet." My words finally click and her body stills, except for her legs. She crosses one over the other and almost loses her balance. I want to knock them apart but that's not where we are in our nonexistent relationship. She's just making it worse on herself.

Putting pressure on your pussy doesn't make the ache subside. It just makes it needier when the pressure is removed. Her breathing has picked up and she lets out a soft moan that is barely coherent. "I won't ask again." She uncrosses her legs and stares at me, saying nothing. I don't beg for anybody so I look her up and down and turn to walk away.

"Kiss me," she says before I can get two steps away. I stop and turn to face her but don't make a move toward her. "Kiss me, please." There you go, she picks up fast. I take my time getting back to her.

"I'm sorry, what was that?" I'm usually not a bitch but she was playing with me and I don't like that. Her eyes fall to the floor and I lift her chin with my pointer finger.

"I want you to kiss me," she says and I smile. I lick my bottom lip and her eyes watch. Slowly I dip my head and capture her mouth with mine. My tongue swipes against her teeth and I feel lumpy gum. Immediate turn-off.

She hasn't chewed on it since she walked in the door. I hate gum. My lip curls down in a disgusted notion and I walk away from her. She probably is thinking that I thought the quick kiss itself was bad. I don't really care.

As much as I thought I needed her before, the feeling is gone. I would rather grind on a pole to get myself off than touch that nasty shit again. What was the point of it even being there if she wasn't chewing it? She stays where I left her and I move on to organizing paperwork behind the counter. I don't look her way for the rest of the time she's here.

Two hours later, I venture out to the showers. I have to check them every couple of hours just to make sure everybody is safe and nobody fell asleep sitting on the floor. Yes, people do that often. They push themselves longer than their body recommends and then pass out once the hot water hits.

Walking in I hear the water from one shower. Nobody else is around, so I go check it out. The curtain is wide the fuck open but I still don't want to walk in. I close my eyes when I am four steps away and call out,

"Hey, you okay in there?" Nobody answers so I try again. "Miss, are you okay?" Still no answer. I open my eyes and take the rest of the steps to where I am directly in front of her, Hasley. She's watching me watch her.

The water is flowing down her pasty white curves, outlining her breasts. Her nipples are rock hard and begging to be bit. I follow the water running down her kissable stomach and wrap around those thighs I imagine taste so fucking good. She takes me off guard when her fingers slide up and pinch her nipples.

"Shit," the word escapes. She bites her bottom lip while she stares at me. Her other hand is between her legs, rubbing her clit. She's making it a show.

"This is a private shower. Mmmm, you don't want to be here anyways," she moans.

"I wouldn't want to be anywhere else. Did you spit that nasty ass gum out?" I ask.

Realization shows on her face. Her fingers haven't stopped when she answers. "Yes, ma'am." As much as I like her calling me that, I would rather do something else. For now, I just want to fuck her. I take long strides until I am under the water with her.

I decided to leave my clothes on, knowing there is an extra set in my locker. I lower my head and place my lips on her neck. I lick, suck, and nibble my way down until I get to her breasts. I pull back and slap her hand away so I can take over.

My eyes lock on her as I take a nipple in my mouth. Both of her hands rest on my shoulders. I suck hard and she squeezes. Her head falls back and the moans get a little higher than a whisper. I wonder if I can make her cum just from this? I will have to try that out one day if I run into her again. I run the tips of my fingers up her inner thigh and cup her pussy.

"You are so wet for me, pet. I'm going to finger fuck you and you are going to be quiet." I give her a second to back out but she doesn't. I slip one finger between her folds and she hisses. I don't take the next movement lightly. I slide my finger into her entrance, feeling her out.

She can handle two fingers with no problem, so I slide another in. I start pumping in her fast and hard. Watching her keep her mouth shut is hot. This is driving her crazy. Her moans are loud enough to where if somebody was in the next stall, they would know what's happening.

She is so sexy. I pull my fingers out of her and make her watch me lick the juices off. She tries to kiss me but I move down to my knees and lift one of her legs over my shoulder. I look at her face one more time and smirk, then I dive into her pussy.

Damn, she tastes sweet. I eat her like I'm starving, lick and suck like she's a fresh peach. Her hands go to my hair and she tugs. I feel my wetness starting to run down my thigh. I need her to cum. I have to get myself off soon.

I slide my middle and ring finger in her and hook it to touch that special spot. Her legs start to shake and her breathing is quick. I push my tongue to her clit and she loses it. She is screaming and pressing her pussy more on my face.

I let her ride it out and when her breathing starts to slow and her legs stop shaking, I stick my tongue inside of her and lick up all of the evidence. When I am satisfied, I slide her leg down and get to my feet. She catches me off guard when she grabs onto my shirt and pulls me in for a kiss. She moans into my mouth and her hand slides down to the waistline of my pants. I pull away just enough to break the kiss.

"I didn't do that for anything in return. I just had to have you," I confess.

"I hope you liked it. I want to know what you feel like," she breathes. I nod my head once and her hand makes its way into the front of my pants and her fingers play with my clit. "I like this. The fact that you are wet because you ate me out. It's turning me on again."

"If you want to do this then do it right. Move your fingers faster. Play with me like the way you play with yourself." I try to talk her through it.

"It's hard to do when I'm facing this way. It hurts my wrist," she says. I turn away from her but hold her arm to keep it in my pants so that she is reaching around. Apparently, this is a better angle because now she is working me like a guitar. It takes no time at all before I'm cumming. I keep my mouth closed but I hear myself groaning.

She is good, so good. She dips her finger inside me and pulls out, waits for me to face her and sticks her fingers in her mouth. Her eyes close and she makes a satisfied sound.

"And you said this was your first time with a girl? You did fucking amazing," I exhale.

Chapter 3

Hasley has come to the gym every day since becoming a member. That was a week ago. I haven't approached her and she hasn't said anything to me. Normally I would be over the moon but it's been a week since I had her in that shower and she is still on my tongue. Fuck, what is wrong with me? I saw her, fucked her and now it's time to move on.

So why do my eyes follow her?

Today she walked in with black leggings that show off her perfect round ass and a white tank top. I've watched her like a creep for the past forty-five minutes and not once had she taken a sip of water. I tell myself to mind my own business. If she wants to pass out from dehydration, let her.

I say that over and over until I can't take it anymore. I march over to her and stand mere inches away. I can smell her strawberry scent and it takes me back to last week. I need her again, but for now, she needs to learn how to take care of herself.

"Can I help you?" she asks me. Her chocolate eyes stare into mine.

"Where is your water bottle? You haven't touched it since you have been here," I ask. Her lip curves up slightly.

"I forgot to bring it," she shrugs. Without a word, I turn and go back to the front desk. I purchase another bottle, fill it up, and take it to her.

"Drink. And next time you forget, tell me," I order.

"Maybe I just wanted you to come up to me," she croons.

"Or you can just come tell me what you want instead of putting yourself in danger. What did you want?" I ask her. She bites down on her lip.

"I was hoping that we can get together again." Her eyes drop to the floor with sudden nerves.

"What are you wanting to happen here?" My expectations aren't high since she can't even walk up to me. She surprises me when she looks dead in my eyes and says,

"I want you to take me home and fuck me." Well, shit. This time it's my turn to let my eyes fall. "I keep thinking about what you did to me. The way you knew exactly where to touch with the perfect amount of pressure. I've never been with a guy who has made me cum. None of them knew what they were doing. But you, you have been on my mind ever since." She gains confidence and gets closer to me so that her nose is almost touching mine. "I went home that night and touched myself. I have been pretending that my fingers have been yours every night. Some mornings I wake up still wet from dreaming of you." When I look back up to her, her eyes are dark and needy. I am fully aware of the people around us and that is the only reason why I don't push her against the equipment and kiss her.

"I can't keep fucking you. I have rules and you won't be able to follow them. What happened between us was a one-time thing. As much as I want to give you exactly what you want, I have to have control," I tell her. The ache between my legs is yelling at me to stop fucking this up. She seems to like what I said because she licks her lips and gives me a look I can only describe as a 'fuck me and tell me I'm a good girl'.

"I can be obedient," she whispers.

"You can't even drink your water, how are you going to do as you're told?" I ask, shaking my head. She comes closer so that her mouth is right by my ear.

"Because the way you worked my pussy in that shower has me wanting to do whatever the fuck you say. I want to know what it feels like laying in your bed. How hard will you finger me when you have space and privacy?" She has me rolling my eyes back, imagining her laid out like a fucking starfish and my handprint on her ass cheek. It takes a minute to regain my composure. "You said a noodle is straight until you get it wet...my water is boiling," she says and licks my ear. Now it's my turn.

"You will call me Mommy and do as you're told. I have to have control over all things in my life but I will not control you while we are out in the real world. I only save that for when we fuck. Do you understand, pet?" It's a long shot but I have to put it all out there before we go any further. She stays quiet for a long minute and I think she is backing out but then she smiles.

"Yes, Mommy," she responds. I wrap her ponytail in my hand and tug her hair back, making her look at me.

"What are your plans tonight?" I ask her. I won't wait for another day to pass before I'm on her again.

"Just soaking in the tub," she answers.

"Get your stuff, we are leaving now." I let her hair go and return to the front counter, collect my things, and tell Jace I'm headed out. Hasley is at the door waiting. That brings a smile to my face. She catches on pretty fast to what I need.

If tonight goes well then we might make this a long-term thing. I head to her and lay my arm over her shoulder then walk out together. We stop at my motorcycle and her mouth drops.

"This is yours?" she squeals, bouncing on her toes.

"Yes, but I wasn't going to make you ride on it. Which one is your car?" Her smile drops which confuses me.

"It's the gray Nissan over there," she answers but disappointment is written all over her face.

"What just happened?" She contemplates answering but thinks better of it and says,

"I wanted to ride on it. My car is boring and this would be fun," she admits. Her eyes catch mine and her bottom lip pokes out in a pout. "Can I please ride on the back...Mommy?" She doesn't need to say anything else, I'm already getting the spare helmet off the hook from under the seat and handing it over to her.

"Are you sure? It can be a bit scary," I ask her one last time before I swing my leg over and sit on the seat. She hopped up without a second thought, putting the helmet on. My hands reach behind and grab her thighs, squeezing. I grab onto the neckline of her helmet and pull it closer to me. "Tightly grab my waist and don't let go." She does exactly that and I throw my helmet on. Satisfied with how she is placed I start my bike up and drive off. Her arms close in around me a bit tighter and I hear her laugh. I love riding, it helps clear my head.

It doesn't take long to make it home, but I never bring people here. It just makes it awkward in the morning. But here we are, in the parking spot of my apartment building. I put my foot on the ground and turn the engine off. We take our helmets off at the same time and she swings her leg over the back to get down.

"That was so much fun! It was so loud and the vibration was very intense," she exclaims, basically jumping up and down. The vibration, huh. That gives me an idea. I slide back to make room up front.

"Get up here," I instruct her and pat the seat between my legs. She hesitates and that irritates me. "Now," I growl. Without another word, she hops on. I pull her shoulders back so she is leaning on me. Looking around, I make sure nobody is watching. It seems clear enough for this.

I run my fingers slowly down her breasts to her stomach. She winces and tries to move away from my touch. Can't have that. I pop her stomach but not too hard. "Move my hand away from it again and you will regret it. Every piece of you is sexy and you will let me worship it." She relaxes against me and my hand slides down into her pants.

I start moving my finger over her clit and she takes a deep breath. I grab her chin with my other hand and tug it upwards and kiss her. She moans in my mouth and I swallow them down. I'm so concentrated on how good her pussy feels I don't hear anybody walk up.

There's a tall fiery redhead clearing her throat. I don't move either of my hands and I keep Hasley's face pointed up to me so that she doesn't see.

"I'm busy, fuck off," I snap. Fuck her for interrupting me. She just smiles and licks her bottom lip.

"I was actually hoping I could help you out with her," she states and I take a minute to think about it.

"What do you think, pet? Do you want to share or keep me all to yourself?" I ask, watching her movements closely. She smiles the biggest fucking smile.

"Another pet? I think I would enjoy that, but only if you want to, Mommy," she responds and I love how open she is. I didn't want to push her anymore today but that girl waiting for an answer is so fucking hot.

"Pull her hair and give her tits attention," I order the new girl. She dives right in like she's done this plenty. And fuck, the sight has me weak. It takes three more flicks and Hasley is shaking and cussing in my mouth.

Damn, she looks so fucking good when she cums. I pull my hand out of her pants but before I can put my fingers in my mouth the other girl grabs my wrist and licks them clean while looking into my eyes. I'm in shock for a moment but recover and grab the back of her neck. I pull her to me.

"That was mine." I lick the side of her face and shove my tongue in her mouth. This kiss has me realizing I can't be happy with just Hasley. I need this one too. Hands find my hips and quick kisses are peppered on my neck. I'm now the cream in our cookie.

"Holy shit," somebody says and it brings me out of my trance. Some kid with wavy black hair and a side lip piercing has his phone out, recording I'm sure. I lick the girls' lips, take Hasley's hand and walk to my door.

"Come on new girl if you want more," I call out to her, not looking to see if she's following.

"Are we going to do things up there?" Hasley asks but there's something in her voice that's off.

"Yes, we are." She better not be backing out. I guess if she does I still have a sexy mystery girl. But I want them both. "What is the problem?" She gnaws on her lip.

"I don't know what to do. You don't have a dick for me to grab." I smile with all my teeth. This is either going to be ridiculously fun or very irritating.

"At the end of the day as long as we are all enjoying ourselves and being safe, that's all that matters. However, I want you naked," I explain to her. The no-name girl walks in and closes the door behind her. "What is your name?"

"Melody, yours?" She asks me.

"Izzy and this is Hasley." Shaking her hand seems like taking five steps back, so I just awkwardly stand there.

"Actually, you can call her 'Mommy'," Hasley jumps in, looking back and forth between us with wide eyes. I don't even know if this chick wants anything more than one night but she doesn't look phased.

"Yes, Ma'am." Melody drops to her knees with her eyes on the floor. *Fuck me*. Hasley looks at her and starts to look anxious. Quickly, she copies and I wish I enjoyed this but it's just not my thing.

"The only time y'all need to be on your knees for me is when I'm cumming in your mouth." They both hurry to their feet.

"I'm sorry, I thought you wanted it. You know, with your Domme name and everything." Melody's shoulders drop with disappointment. Why do I even care? I just want to play with her like a toy but the people pleaser in me has me wanting to give her what she wants.

"Strip and go to the couch, both of you," I demand and they obey. I take a deep breath, clear my head, roll my shoulders back, tilt my chin down, and follow behind them. Hasley looks extremely uncomfortable so I stand in front of her first. I bend over and put my hands on either side of her, supporting myself with the couch.

She tenses and I kiss the top of her head, she relaxes under my lips. My lips drag down her face to her jaw and I plant a kiss there. I can feel her breath on me and I love it. I slide to her ear and nibble on her earlobe. She hums with excitement. Mmm, that sound. I want to hear it every day. Wait, no I don't. What the fuck has this girl done to me? *Hell no.*

"I'm going to get on my knees for you and you're going to scoot to the edge of the seat. You are going to put that pretty pussy in my face and I'm going to eat you like no man has done. And, you're going to want more by the time I'm done," I whisper in her ear. I drop on one knee and then on the other. Her eyes are hooded and I can see that she wants this. She does what I say and I get a good look at what I'm about to devour. She's glistening. Her wetness is leaking out and I lick it up before it runs down her ass.

"Melody, touch yourself while you watch," I say without looking away from my meal. I bury my face in her and inhale that sweet scent. "Watch me, watch what I am doing to you." I spread her legs further apart and hold them there as I take a long drag of my tongue to her. She shivers and that's my sign to keep going. I hear the slapping sound of Melody fingering herself and fuck she sounds wet. I lick, suck, and nibble on her until her legs are shaking and then I push two fingers into her warm entrance. She comes undone and her thighs are squeezing my head. Her moans are loud and sexy. I keep licking until her spasms stop, wipe my mouth, and look over at Melody.

"I wanted to know what it feels like so I decided to wait," Melody says. I give her a smirk and slide over to her. She is already on the edge of the couch and has her legs wide open for me. It's obvious that she has done this a time or two. Luckily, I'm confident. I start eating her as one would dive into a peach, she's juicy like one too. When she cums, her hands go to my head and push me closer to her. She rotates her hips while she rides out her orgasm. Once done, I stand and head to my bathroom. I still need a shower.

I have spent three days between their thighs, my face in their breasts, and my hand on their asses. I'm fucking tired. I had to set a timer on my phone for us to take a water and snack breaks. I sent Melody home and drove Hasley to hers in my car this time.

I need some space to think. Do I want this just to be a one-time meet-up? Do I want to only fuck them? Or do I want to make this an actual thing?

We spent very little time resting and talking, but the conversations that did happen were amazing. They are both funny and sweet. Melody has a snappy side to her, whereas Hasley is so innocent. Even if I wanted to keep both, is that something they would want too?

My head is pounding even after the Tylenol. Maybe I should send a group text asking them to be mine. *What? No, not a fucking text. That's stupid.* I'll just tell them to meet me somewhere public.

Chapter 4

The bar is crowded and that is perfect. Plenty of people to hide me if one of the girls goes ape-shit. I sit at a table with my water and white freezie, waiting. I wanted to sit here and think before they showed up. So I made my way over here a little early.

I was going to order them drinks but I don't know what they like, I did get them water though. I lean my head back on the bench and close my eyes. It would be amazing to keep both of them. I'm deep in thought when I hear Hasley.

"Mommy, are you okay?" She sits on the other side of the table and slides all the way in. Melody sits beside her. They are both wearing light jackets to accommodate the September chill nipping in the air, and all I can think about is getting them off and touching, sucking, and kissing what's underneath. *Fuck...*

"What would y'all like to drink? Everything is on me." I decided to go ahead and get the small talk out of the way. Melody stares into my eyes and her left brow arches in a questioning gesture. I guess they aren't interested in it and want to get to the point. I take a deep breath and spill. "I want to keep both of you. Not just for sex but for everything. I believe we had a great time and would like to explore that." I first look at Hasley to watch for a reaction. She smiles and nods her head.

"I was really nervous at first but y'all made me feel amazing. I never felt like that with any of the guys that I've been with. They just wanted to get theirs but y'all took the time to make sure I felt good. *Really* good. I want that. I like how much you pay attention to the little details. I don't want to sound desperate but I need this," she whimpers and her eyes start to water.

Melody wraps her arms around Hasley's shoulders and squeezes then kisses the top of her head. It takes a minute but she dries her eyes and pulls away.

Melody opens up, "I think that would be a great idea. I loved being with both of you, it was fun and refreshing. Izzy, I need you to be who you are because I need a place where I don't have to think or make decisions. I have to be on my A-game constantly and with you taking over, it's like a weight being lifted off my shoulders. All in all, I think we should do it. Are we going to be exclusive or do we play with other people?"

"You need more than two women to fuck?" I ask her. I don't know if I could allow them to be open with others.

"All I need is right here at this table. I just want to make sure everything is said aloud so there are no gray areas and it's out there." She giggles after she says that. I finally breathe. *Have I been holding it that whole time?*

"We can not be involved with anybody else. It will just be us. We don't have to do everything together all the time. For example, y'all can fuck each other without me or go eat together. All dates will be for the three of us. If y'all have any fantasies then just tell me and I will do my best to make it happen. I also would like a paper on what is a no-go. I don't want either of you to feel uncomfortable," I clarify. "Now, what would you like to drink?"

We spent the rest of the day together and didn't have sex, not once. I learned that Melody's grandma used to be trained at the gym by Jace. Crazy how small this world is. She also works at a tattoo shop. I don't have any artwork on me but I might let her do a little something.

She went to college and majored in art. Makes sense. Hasley is a plant collector and doesn't bring them home just to die. Good for her because my thumb can't be any more black.

She also has a passion for reading, maybe she can hang out with Ash and become friends. Hopefully they read the same type of books because I would love for her to learn a few things. I tell them about myself and how I'm not about punishment or anything like that. I just like to be in control, I have to be or I will go insane.

Melody seems excited about that. I can understand the need to rest your brain for a little bit but I don't get that privilege. I also found out Melody used to have a problem with self-medicating. She is 5 years clean but still struggles.

I will have to research this because I don't know much about those things but I will support and help her in any way I can. Hasley is open to this new relationship. It's actually very surprising because I have put two new things in front of her. She now has to submit to me, a woman.

It's going to be difficult for her I'm sure. Men have never treated her well and it shows in how much she puts herself down. She looks fucking incredible and I can't wait to show her that every single day.

I sent them home after dinner so they can have some alone time to think about if they really want this. It's easy to say you want something when it is right in front of you but give them a night alone and that can change. I need them to be in this completely, not one foot in and one foot out the door. I text them about 30 minutes after they leave.

PETS GROUP CHAT

> ME: did you make it home

> Melody: Yes.

> Hasley: Yes, ma'am.

> ME: you dont have to call me that unless we are fucking

> Hasley: I know but I like it. Is that ok?

> ME: thats fine, I just wanted you to know

I usually go to the bar at night but since I have 2 girls, I don't need to try with other people. I need to slow down on the alcohol anyways because Melody has made it clear that she doesn't want to drink. She said she doesn't have a problem with it but she doesn't want to go from one addiction to another. I can understand that and support it.

I'm getting too old for the parties and shit anyway. I get bored in my tiny place so I decide to get ready for bed.

My bathroom smells like Hasley - strawberry. It is actually everywhere but I ignore it.

I take my time brushing my teeth, then my hair. I usually don't wash my face but I guess it's time to start. Wrinkles are starting to appear in the corner of my eyes. Of course I don't know how to splash water on my face without getting it all over the counter. Looks like a damn tsunami.

Taking a towel and wiping it up I notice my towel closet is bare now. Okay, I can do some laundry instead of sleeping. I'm not tired anyway. Just then my phone starts ringing. It's Jace.

"Hello?"

"She's fucking crazy."

"I feel like that is what you wanted."

"Not like this. She started crying because all the Skittles were gone. She doesn't like Skittles."

"That is hilarious. Guess you better go to a bulk store and get a few cases."

I load the washing machine with a load of dirty clothes while the phone is between my shoulder and ear. I need to invest in some headphones.

"So, do you want to hang out with her? Not at the bar or coffee shop but at your place?"

"Ha, nope. Your baby, your problem. I don't do those emotions."

"You're the fucking best, thank you. I just need an hour of quiet."

"What are you going to do when the baby gets here and all you hear is that little shit crying?"

"That's where aunt Izzy comes in."

"That's fucking adorable. Maybe one of my girlfriends likes kids and can help."

I take my conversation to the couch and cover myself with a throw blanket.

"Should I be questioning the girlfriend part or that you have more than one?"

"I can't be happy with just one person and these two girls like us being together. Also, the sex is incredible."

"Don't you get tired of pleasing both of them?

"Like making them cum? They can do it to each other as well. Plus, I enjoy it. You can't tell me you haven't watched lesbian porn."

"Yeah but that's all for show. It's their job. Just saying it seems like a lot of work to satisfy both of them."

"If you can't make your fiancée cum, just say so. I can give you some pointers."

"Ha-fucking-ha. I am more than enough for her. But if there was another with her, nope."

"Where is she now? I hear no crying."

"I ran her a bath. She is also mad she can't sit in a tub of lava. I tried but can't get used to having a thousand-degree water running down my body."

"Maybe that will put her in a better mood or at least distract her."

"I got to go but thanks for nothing. You fucking suck."

He hangs up on me and I let my head drop back and rest on the couch. I am so glad I don't have to deal with that. It's still early but today was long so I think I'm going to go to bed. When I get to my room I strip and crawl into bed. I sleep naked because it is freeing. I do get a bit cold but that's what blankets are for. It doesn't take long before I pass out.

I wake up to a few messages but I don't want to open them and start my day just yet, so I lay there with my eyes closed for another 15 minutes. I finally pry myself off the bed and go pee. My bladder is the enemy. I go back to my room and check my phone.

PETS GROUP CHAT

Hasley: Good morning!

Melody: You don't have to be so excited about it. It's too early for that shit.

Hasley: You didn't have to wake up and respond. I didn't force you.

Melody: The message notification is really loud for this group.

ME: good morning

Hasley: Are we hanging out today?

ME: do you have something that you want to do

Melody: I could think of a few things, ma'am.

ME: i will be home all day, come over whenever you want.

> **Hasley:** I'm getting in my car now! See you in a minute!

> **Melody:** I can join for a couple of hours but I have to ink somebody's arm a little later.

I make up my bed quickly and make some breakfast - pancakes and bacon. I want to throw some eggs in there but I'm all out. My grocery list is starting to get lengthy. I'm almost done flipping the cakes and there's a knock on my door.

The smile that coats my face is stupidly big. I can't help it, those girls make me happy. Even their spats are cute to witness. I open the door to Hasley, she has on a yellow, flowy sundress with thick spaghetti straps. Her hair is down but straightened. She is wearing light makeup, just a swipe of mascara and a touch of lip gloss.

I immediately kiss it all off, still standing in the doorway. She starts giggling and I pull her inside. Not long after she gets settled on the couch, there's another knock. Hasley jumps up and skips to the door.

"Oh, sorry. Can I answer it? I assume it's Melody," she asks. I just smile and stack pancakes on the 3 plates.

"Go for it," I answer her. I hear 2 sets of giggles. There's a smacking sound and then a yelp.

"Melody! That stung!" Hasley yells out then laughs.

"Good. Just rub it and it will go away," Melody tells her.

"No, Melody. Aftercare is important. You soothe her ass," I scold her. I pull the bacon from the pan and evenly distribute them.

"That smells really good. Where do we sit to eat?" Melody asks. I simply point to the couch.

"I don't have a table because it's usually just me. Also, there's no room. The coffee table is enough," I respond. Melody picks up 2 plates and takes them to the table, Hasley gets the other. I pull out the forks and syrup.

"What do y'all want to drink? I have sweet tea, milk, orange juice, and water." I pull out glasses and pour myself some tea. I drink so much tea it's more than likely in my bloodstream. Melody wants water and Hasley asks for orange juice. I make a mental note for next time. We sit and eat in silence, somewhat. Melody is making everything sexual and I can't take my eyes off her, but I won't touch her until everybody is done with their food.

"I poured way too much syrup," Melody realizes.

"Oh, here. Let me help," Hasley pipes in and lowers her head to the plate. She runs her tongue over it and licks up the deep gold stickiness. When she sits back up, she has a little on her lips and Melody licks that off. These girls are the sexiest people. Fuck.

"Eat," I burst their bubble.

"I fully intend to, ma'am," Melody is hard to resist. She knows what she wants and is not afraid to go for it in full force.

"Your food," I scold and her face falls. They quickly finish and wait for me to tell them it's okay to jump each other. I just roll my eyes.

"Go ahead. I'll join after I finish cleaning these dishes up." I grab the plates and take them to the sink. I haven't made it back to get the cups and I hear loud moaning. Good, they can go ahead and get one out before I get there. Hasley is still learning but she still needs to practice more.

Everybody has their own way of eating so it isn't about doing it exactly right, it's about being confident in what you are doing. If you are questioning yourself then the person can feel it with the slowness, softness, and the way your tongue doesn't know where to go. I finish the dishes and lay them out to dry, and head to the bedroom. Hasley is between Melody's thighs. She's trying but Melody just looks frustrated. I take my clothes off and straddle Hasley's back. I lean down so that my face is next to hers.

"Pet, she isn't even wet. All of this is from your spit. Did you warm her up or just get right to it?" I ask. Her sad face says it all. She skipped foreplay. "Watch and take notes. Put a smile back on your face. This is new and I am not trying to put you down. I just want to teach you." She gives me a half-ass smile and nods her head. That's good enough for me. I get off her and crawl up to Melody. I start kissing her softly and slowly push my tongue in between her lips.

They do a little dance while my hand makes its way down to her boob and pinches her nipple. She moans in my mouth and I bite her bottom lip. I watch her lips curve into a smile and I lick her mouth. I kiss her cheek, jaw, and stop at her neck. I bite it but not hard enough to make a mark.

She squirms underneath me and I hold her still. She likes the pain, I can play with that. After spending a minute or two I kiss from her neck, down her chest, and to her boobs. She has a nice C cup and they are perfectly round.

I nibble on the swells and lick over her nipple before biting it. Her hands try to touch her pussy but I grab her wrist and pull it over her head. She catches her lip between her teeth and looks down at me. I move to the other side and show it the same attention.

My mouth slides down her side until I get to her hips and I nip that too. She moans out. I sit up on my knees and grab her ankle. Slowly, I lick up her leg and stop when I get to the top of her thigh. I lay back down on my stomach and look her in her eyes when I bury my face in her now wet and juicy pussy. Her back arches and Hasley crawls over to take Melody's nipple in her mouth.

"Oh My God, Yes! Fuck. Bite, Hasley, bite!" She moans loudly. I grab onto the outside of her thighs to keep them spread apart as she starts to shake.

"Shit. I'm cumming, I'm cumming," she chants. Her hand is on the back of my head pushing me to her even more. When she stops shaking my tongue darts into her entrance and takes the juices I worked for. I lick her pussy one last time and sit up. Melody stays still, catching her breath. Hasley has her hand between her own legs. I slap it away.

"Stop that, you're supposed to be going crazy." I lean in to kiss her but she puts her hand up to stop me. Did I cross a line that I for some reason haven't had a discussion about? Damnit, I know better than to just fuck freely, but before I can make the decision to move on, she moves in and starts kissing my neck. The wetness of her tongue slides down to my boobs and she plays with them.

Her lips clasp around my nipple and the other is occupied with her hand. I let out a slight hum that encourages her to keep going. Melody slides over and starts kissing me. She has her tongue down my throat and I slip my hand between her thighs and start to play with her clit.

She moans in my mouth, the vibration sending a sweet sensation down my spine. Hasley moves down to my hip and places sloppy kisses all around but doesn't touch my pussy. It's like she's teasing me. Good, I like it. I try to stay still but my hips move anyway.

Her mouth finds my entrance and she pushes her tongue in, and pulls it out just to stick it back where it belongs. She does that a couple more times and then finds my clit. There's sucking and nibbling. It's driving me crazy. I push Melody off of me so that I can look down at Hasley. I wrap her hair around my fist and pull her back.

"Fucking eat me," I demand. She smiles, obviously feeling very proud of herself. My hand loosens and I push her face to me. Once her tongue starts, I go insane. My head falls back and Melody's lips are on my nipples.

"Yes, yes, yes. Right there. Fuck! Keep going, Hasley. Yes, fuck me, Hasley," I moan loudly. It only takes me a minute and I'm cumming all over her face. Damn, that was good. She slows her movements as I come down from ecstasy. Melody sits up and watches Hasley with heated eyes. "Melody, lay on your back." She does as she's told. "Hasley, sit on her face." She looks at me like I'm crazy.

"I can't, I'll crush her," she says. Melody reacts before I can.

"Sit on my fucking face so that I can eat you and all of your cum can run down my throat."

"Say something about your weight again and I will slap your ass until it's redder than that lace you wore last week," I snapped at her. She has to stop that shit.

Melody grabs her and pulls her to her face. Hasley straddles, Melody grabs her thighs and pulls her to sit down. While they get started, I crawl to Melody's legs and slide between them. My tongue goes straight to her little bud. She moans into Hasley's pussy and the vibration from it has Hasley bent over with her hands on the bed.

"Oh, shit. Fuck me, yes," Hasley yells. Melody is right behind her and they are cumming undone together. We keep it up until they calm down. All three of us fall to the mattress, worn out.

"Wow, that was really good," Hasley says, out of breath.

"You did a great job, Hasley. Keep that shit up," I compliment her. I fall asleep, satisfied.

Chapter 5

Monday gets here faster than I wanted. I drag myself out of bed and turn the shower on. I absolutely hate mornings but I need the money. This shitty apartment has high rent.

I pull my hair back so it doesn't get wet, I will wash it tonight. Stepping into the water is like heaven. The warmth trailed down my body, relaxing my muscles. After standing there a few minutes, I turn it off and step out, wrapping a towel around my body.

That didn't help wake me up at all. I think it made me even more tired. Looks like I'll be stopping for coffee. I rush to get dressed and run out of the door. Monday mornings are always crazy at Ash's.

Nobody will notice or even care if I'm late but I care. Being on time is what gets me there before lunchtime. I drive there and it's just what I thought, a line out of the damn door. I look at my phone for the first time this morning and see the text messages but ignore them for now.

I call Ash to see if she can make mine and give it to me around back. Of course, she says she can but that will be an extra fifteen dollars. I tell her I will buy extra diapers and she laughs. I drive around to her and she looks so tired.

"Hey, babe. What's wrong," I ask her. Her eyes start to water and I try to hug her but she pushes me away.

"If you hug me then the waterworks will start and they won't stop. It's these fucking hormones. Poor Jace is trying but he's so fucking hot, I start crying when I see him naked. He's beautiful," she says and it freaks me out.

"Okay, well thank you for the coffee…" I try to walk away but she stops me.

"You never sent back your RSVP," she says. What the hell is she talking about?

"Sweetheart, I never got one. I figured y'all knew that I would be there." She should know that I wouldn't miss their wedding for the world.

"Yeah but I need to know who you are bringing if anybody," she catches an attitude but I keep my cool.

"I will let you or Jace know by the end of the day. I may be bringing two. Would that be okay?" I ask.

"Two? Yeah, that's fine. I'm happy for you. I will be highly disappointed if I don't catch y'all fucking there," she jokes… I think. But she looks pretty serious. I turn and get back in my car. Nope, not touching that one. I heard how horny pregnant people are.

I wait until she is back in the shop before I drive off. She is crazy, that's the only thing I can say about that conversation. The parking lot of the gym is packed too. That's odd, nobody wants to work out this early on a Monday.

I park and walk through the glass door. Almost every machine is occupied. The heavy ropes are even being used. Did I miss something? I see Jace working with a guy and I call him over.

"First of all, your girl is fucking nuts. Secondly, where did all of these people come from?" I am trying to wrap my mind around this but I feel like I'm missing something.

"Don't tell her because she will flip the fuck out. I looked at her wrong last night and she swore I was cheating on her with some girl in my dreams. I don't even remember my dreams. But these people? Yeah, I don't know actually. I know one family just moved down the road but I couldn't tell you about the rest. I'll catch up with you later, I got to stretch my client out," he says as he walks away. I take my coffee to the counter and pull my phone out of my pocket.

PETS GROUP CHAT

> **Hasley:** Good morning! I hope that woke you up, Melody.

> **Melody:** No worries, it fucking did.

> **Hasley:** Awe, poor baby.

> **Melody:** Go fuck yourself.

> **Hasley:** Or you can come over here and fuck me.

> **Melody:** Don't fucking play with me. I will be there in less than five minutes.

> **Hasley:** I dare you.

> **Melody:** On my way!

Well shit. I didn't think they would be at it this early. I know I told them that they can do whatever without me but I feel left out. I send out a quick text.

> **ME:** can I at least get a picture so I feel like I'm there

It takes a few minutes but Melody sends one to me. She's laying down with her legs wide. The angle that it is taken from is what she sees. Hasley is eating her while looking into the camera.

I feel the need build up and I push my thighs together. Yeah, it only makes the feeling more intense but what else am I supposed to do? I send them a picture of me with my tongue out and tell them to get a couple of licks in for me. After that, I put my phone away and start work.

There is a mountain of paperwork from all of the people that just signed up this morning. It's insane. While I'm putting the information on the computer, I think about Hasley and Melody. I never thought I would be happy in an exclusive relationship. I guess I feel okay with it since it's two people instead of being dedicated to only one.

The morning passes in a blur and I haven't heard from my girls'. They are probably at work. Melody starts around lunchtime and Hasley runs a music store that opens at ten. It's funny that she works with music and is dating somebody named Melody. It's like we are meant to be. I shoot out a quick text just to check in.

PETS GROUP CHAT

> **ME: how are yall doing today**
>
> **Hasley: It's actually pretty dead here.**
>
> **ME: maybe because they are all at the gym**
>
> **Hasley: Ouch. I actually wish we could have a few people here. This just makes time go by so slowly.**
>
> **ME: i guess that's true i'm going to get back to it but I wanted to check-in**

Melody must be tattooing somebody. She will text me when she can. I never have to worry about that. I put my phone in the side pocket of my leggings and start wiping down empty equipment.

Hasley is right, the crazy makes the day go by faster. My shift is over in the blink of an eye. Today was so busy I didn't think to check my phone. I pull it out of my pocket and there are texts in the group.

PETS GROUP CHAT

Melody: I'm taking a break from the sleeve that I've been doing.

Hasley: Maybe I can talk you into giving me a little tattoo.

Melody: You won't have to do much. It will probably turn you on.

Hasley: It didn't make me feel that way with the other one.

Melody: Yeah but what if we can beg Izzy to lick you while I do it?

Hasley: That sounds a lot more enjoyable.

Melody: I got to get back to this guy's arm.

I like that there's no awkwardness between them. It just seems natural and flows easily. I shoot back a quick text.

> **ME:** sorry I wasn't responding. today was a lot. i can definitely taste you while you are doing anything. i have a question for yall but I want to ask in person, its nothing bad but i don't want to do this over the phone

> **Hasley:** Ok, well that doesn't give me anxiety at all…

> **Melody:** That's not nice.

> **ME:** come over whenever yall can

I gather my things and head home. When I get there, a few kids are outside playing what looks like freeze tag. I'm a little jealous of how they have nothing weighing on them. They can run and play without a care in the world.

"Hey, Ms. Izzy," a little girl says. She told me her name before but I forgot what it was. Her wavy black hair is pulled up in a pony tale and her creamy brown skin is flawless. She's in a cute pink sundress. I squat down until I'm at eye level.

"Hey, sweetheart. How are you doing?" I ask her.

"Good. A girl keeps picking on me," she informs me.

What the hell?

"Who?" I keep my composure but I can't stand a bully. Kid or not.

"She isn't out here today but she says that nobody likes me because my mom is a police officer," she tells me.

"Do you think nobody likes you? It looks like you have friends all around you trying to play." I look around at the rest of the kids.

"They all play with me. So maybe she's lying." That brings her smile back to life and I stand up. I give her a fist bump and wink, then walk to my apartment. I am in desperate need of a shower. Hasley is standing at my door. How the hell did she get here so fast? There are worry lines between her brows.

"Hey, pet." I greet her with a smile that she doesn't return.

"You can't do that with me. I have anxiety about everything," she tells me and is visibly shaking.

"I was going to ask if y'all want to be my plus two for my best friend's wedding. Okay? So calm down," I tell her and unlock my front door. She follows me inside and I hear her breathing slow down. I help her to the couch and sit beside her.

"That was it? Just about the wedding? Nothing else?" She spits out the questions fast.

"Yes, that was it. I wanted to ask in person so I can gauge your reaction. I didn't want any of you to feel like y'all had to. I would never text you anything bad or keep you hanging. I promise. Now, do you want some water?" I ask while I rub her arm. She just nods and I get up to get it for her.

"I'm sorry, I don't mean to be crazy. I just get really nervous and it takes a minute to get myself together." Her eyes are fixed on the floor as she talks.

"Hey, stop it. Don't ever be embarrassed with me. I will never do that to you again. I don't want you to feel that way because of me." I'm interrupted by a knock on the door. I go to see who it is through the peephole. Melody. I open the door for her and step to the side so she can come in.

"So what was so important that couldn't be said over the phone?" she says with a little bitch in her tone.

"Watch it, pet," I use a stern tone to remind her where her place is. She turns away from me and goes to sit beside Hasley.

"None of us are naked so we are in the everyday dynamic." She got me there. I did say that. It is becoming a bit harder than I had thought. I wouldn't classify myself as a Domme and them as subs. It just turns me on when they are at my disposal.

"My friend is getting married and I wanted to know if y'all want to be my plus two?" I ask. Melody has her hair in a fishtail braid and has some eye makeup on. It's bright-ass blue with a perfect eyeliner wing. That takes serious skill on its own. When I try it, my eyes look like cousins instead of twins.

"When is it?" Melody questions with an irritated look. I now understand that I made a serious mistake with that text. Never again.

"It's in two weeks, on a Saturday," I start fidgeting with my fingernails as this conversation is starting to make me nervous.

"The music store is closed on weekends so I can be there. I'll just need to go find a dress," Hasley responds first.

"Yeah, I can. I'll just request that day off. We are only closed on Sundays. My schedule is different every week but this is plenty of time to get their shit straight," Melody says and lets out a puff of air. Hearing their answers allows my muscles to relax, which I didn't know were tense to begin with.

"I'll let my friend know. I stink so I'm taking a shower. Make yourselves at home, I'll be right back." That being said, I head to my shower and turn it on. I stand there, arms pressed into the countertop, holding me up and I focus on my breathing. Steam starts spilling over the curtain and I remove my clothes. My back hurts from all of the bending over at work. Why don't people clean their space after they finish? It only takes a second.

I step in the shower and let the scorching water run down my aching back. I have to put my hands on the tile wall to keep myself from falling. Nothing has happened but my emotions get the best of me and tears start falling, mixing with the water from the shower. My period is due any day now and I have been ignoring the slight cramps today. I'll have to make a store run when I get out, I'm completely out of tampons.

Normally I am more prepared but those girls have set me off of my normal routine. I allow myself to cry for a minute and get it together - wash my hair, face, and body. When I get out I feel drained and just want to go to bed. I know they are going to fuck but I'm not feeling it. Maybe they can scratch that itch while I'm gone. I leave the bathroom and go to my room, leaving the door open behind me. Melody and Hasley strut in after me before my towel hits the floor.

"What's wrong," Hasley asks. Of course, she notices. She sees everything.

"Nothing, my period is due any day now. I'm gonna get dressed and head to the store. Do y'all need anything?" I ask while I dry off.

"Stay here and I will get stuff for you," Hasley orders and I roll my eyes.

"I'm the one that is supposed to take care of y'all, not the other way around." It seems wrong for them to do things for me. Nobody's ever even offered.

"Here, lay down and I'll give you a massage while she gets some tampons and chocolate." Melody takes my towel and starts drying my hair. I hum in approval. Fuck that feels so relaxing.

"I'll be right back. What kind of wine do you like?" Hasley is almost out of my room but I stop her.

"No wine. I don't drink anymore and it won't be in this house," I try to keep my voice nonchalant but Melody picks up on it.

"You don't have to do that. My problems shouldn't stop you from anything you want to do." She's out of her mind if she thinks that way. I grab her chin and tug her closer to my face.

"You are mine. Do you understand me? I will respect and support you. I won't do anything that will lead you astray." My face is serious when I tell her and I make sure she looks me in the eyes. They need to learn that this relationship is not like the others.

"Thank you," is all she says, and Hasley leaves. I get in bed and lay on my stomach. Melody straddles right above my ass. She starts to rub my back and then stops. I whine at the sudden coldness of her hands leaving me.

"I'm going to get some lotion, be right back." She moves off but is back within seconds. I feel the pressure of her settling back into position and hear her warming the lotion in her hands before I feel it on my shoulders. She starts out slow and light but adds some pressure into it and it feels amazing. I moan and I start to doze off. I wake up to her still straddling me but her top half is laying on my back. I can tell she is shirtless.

"I'm sorry I fell asleep. That just felt so good and I couldn't help it," I apologize. She lets out a small laugh and kisses the center of my back.

"It's okay, I'm happy that I can relax you. I like the way your skin feels on me." She starts to stroke my hair and I swear I'm in heaven.

"How long was I out? Is Hasley back?" I ask, hearing the roughness in my voice. *I hope I didn't snore.*

"Only thirty minutes. Hasley dropped everything off but went home." She gets off me as she speaks and it worries me.

"Is she okay?" I quickly sit up on my knees. Melody is putting her bra and shirt back on.

"Yeah, she said she wanted to go ahead and eat so that she could unwind and get ready for bed. Something about having to get up early to get some work in at the gym." She shakes her head while she tells me. I grab my phone and send her a text.

> **ME: im sorry that i fell asleep are you ok**

> Hasley: Yeah, I just wanted to get home.

> ME: that sounds off. whats going on

> Hasley: Nothing

> ME: dont do that with me

> Hasley: This is still all new to me. Not only do I have a GIRLfriend but I'm sharing you with somebody else. It's a lot.

Damnit.

> ME: i know. what do you need from me so i can help

> Hasley: First off, can you start using English? It drives me crazy reading your messages.

ME: Really? I'm sorry. It's just quicker to type it without worrying about all the punctuation and shit. But for you, I will work on it.

Hasley: Thank you. I just need some time to get used to it all. TIME, NOT SPACE. So don't leave me out of anything.

ME: I can do that. Maybe the three of us can go out for dinner Friday night.

Hasley: Are you asking me out on a first date?

ME: Yes, I am.

Hasley: I will have to look at my calendar.

Hasley: I'm a busy woman.

ME: Go out with me and I will give you something else you can busy yourself with.

> **Hasley:** So tempting...
>
> **Hasley:** Yes, you can count me in!

> **ME:** Perfect. Good night, pet.

She likes me calling her that so I do it as often as I can, just to make her feel good. Melody doesn't need reassurance so I don't do it with her.

"Is she okay, like I said?" I hear Melody ask and I look up to see her standing across the room with her hands on her hips.

"Actually, she was feeling overwhelmed with everything. She's fine now. Would you like to go on a date Friday night?" I leave the bed and go to the bathroom, waiting for her answer.

"Can it be a late one? I don't have to stay until the shop closes but Friday nights are usually busy and I kinda want the business," she has confidence in her question. It's one reason why I like her so much, she carries herself well.

"That's fine. How late are we talking?" We aren't to the point where we feel comfortable peeing in front of each other so we are talking through the bathroom door. It's ridiculous because we have seen every part of each other but this is so taboo it feels different.

"I don't know. Maybe ten?" I'm not sure why but the tone she uses sounds like she has an attitude. I finish up and wash my hands, still walking around naked.

"What's the problem, Melody?" I keep the space between us but I'm staring her down. I'm not a fucking kid and I'm not dealing with all of this shit.

"Just think about me when y'all make plans. Tattoo shops open later in the day and close late at night. Sundays are the only nights that I can do things. Every time I have to take off or leave early, I lose money. I'm not struggling but that's because I work my ass off." She lets out a nervous breath after her little breakdown. I close the space between us and take her hands in mine.

"You are completely right. I was thinking about me and my schedule. We don't have to do Friday night. How about Sunday breakfast?" I suggest and bring her hands up to my lips and give them a kiss.

"Since Hasley has to suffer by not going Friday night, how about Saturday morning?" She compromises and I smile. This is going to work, I can feel it. My girls are starting to think about the three of us, and not just what has been ingrained into them for years, where only two people can be in a relationship at once. These girls are my everything, I would do anything for them.

"I'll let her know. That will give us all morning together and you'll still have time to get to work." I give her my sweetest smile to coax her back into a good mood. She smiles back and rolls her eyes, giving me a small breathy laugh. I lean in slowly just in case she doesn't want to but she meets me halfway and we give an innocent kiss.

"Text me when you make it home, please," I whisper and she pulls away, turning towards the door and closing it behind her. The apartment is now quiet and I don't think I like it. I'm used to having them here, laughing and moaning. I get in bed and pull the covers to my neck. I stay awake long enough to get the text from Melody and I pass out, again.

Chapter 6

I woke up to my period. I knew it would happen and I should have been prepared but I still don't like it. I take a quick shower and pull my sheets off of the bed, stain-treat them, throw them in the washer, and get ready for work. I take a look at my phone but there are no messages. That's weird because I always wake up to Hasley and Melody arguing.

PETS GROUP CHAT

> **ME: Good morning, Pets**

> **Melody: Good morning.**

I wait for a few minutes but Hasley doesn't message back. Maybe her workout is distracting. But why wouldn't she text me when she got up? I put my phone in my pocket and head out the door.

I get there in no time and Hasley's car is at the back of the lot but she's not in there. Why would she park all the way in the back? I don't like whatever the hell is going on with her. I park my car in my spot and turn the engine off. It looks pretty empty which is a relief since yesterday was so crazy.

I walk into the building and stop dead in my tracks. She's talking to Jace and it looks serious. I go straight for them. Jace looks up to see me and his smile appears. That man is always smiling. Hasley looks up as I approach and she looks sad.

"Hey, what's going on? You didn't text me this morning," I begin, looking at her and Jace slowly backs away until he is out of our bubble and walks away as fast as he can.

"I'm not the only one that can start the morning chain, you can too," she snaps at me. That takes me back but I keep myself under control.

"I actually did text the group this morning but you never responded," I say back.

"Oh, my phone is in my bag. I must have put it on silent." She still looks like something is up. She shifts from one foot to the other and I can't hold my tongue anymore.

"Is there a problem because I can't keep doing this pouting thing? I'm too old for it."

"You canceled our date for Friday night," I swear her bottom lip pokes out when she says it.

"Seriously? That's your problem?" I take a step back, cross my arms and laugh, shaking my head at her. "Get yourself together. Melody works late that night and as I said before, we go on dates – together. If you can't do Saturday morning then we cancel the whole damn thing. But I will NOT walk on eggshells in my relationship. That's one of the reasons I have stayed single for so long. Do you understand?" I tried not to but my voice was rougher than I wanted. Her eyes start to water and I feel bad so I pull her into my arms and hold her. I'm not sorry I said it but I could have waited until later and definitely in a better tone.

"I'm sorry, I don't know why I'm like this. I'm just so scared that y'all will grow closer and I'll be the third wheel. I've been left behind before and it doesn't feel good," she cries into my neck. I pat her back and stroke her hair.

"Stop this. I will not baby you. Look at me. You won't get anywhere with me by crying. I will treat the two of you differently because y'all are different. Melody doesn't need reassurance so I won't give it to her. You don't need to be under my control all the time, so I won't do that to you. I feel like I am being fair. I haven't fucked either of you alone but y'all have without me. What if I said I am feeling set aside?" She shakes her head back and forth quickly with concern on her face. "But I'm not because I'm an adult and I know better. Are you going to keep being jealous?" I ask her and hope she says she'll try to keep herself in line.

"I will do my best. When I start thinking that way again, I'll just walk up and kiss you like I need it to breathe." A flirty smile growing on her face.

The gym members are watching us but they are trying to be sneaky about it. A wet dream for most of them, two women arguing add some jello or mud in the mix and they would probably blow their load on the spot. I pull back and kiss her forehead.

"Now, go work out. I have to see what's waiting for me behind the counter but I will come to help you out once I finish," I inform her and spin her away from me, gently slap her ass and send her on her way. She turns to look at me and her cheeks are flushed

"Do you like that?" My voice just above a whisper.

"Yes, Mommy," she says and I have to close my eyes to try and keep myself together. When my eyes open, she's smirking, then turns and walks away. She likes to get spanked, that gives me an idea. I walk to my spot behind the counter and pull my phone out. I look up riding crops. I order two and put my phone away.

Oh, this is going to be fun. I wonder what else she likes. *Can I tie her up? Maybe use a spreader bar.* I shake my head to try and bring myself back to the real world. My thoughts have made my pussy wet. My thighs are sticky and I just want to drag her to the showers and make her kneel. I need to stop and focus.

Surprisingly, there are no new sign-ups but I do need to make sure there aren't any monthly payments overdue. I'm trying to concentrate but I keep looking up to watch Hasley. I know I shouldn't but I want her. *Patience*. I put my focus back on the computer and get some emails sent out for upcoming bills.

It takes 2 hours to get everything caught up but once I'm done, I walk straight to Hasley. I've been keeping an eye on her, watching her work her legs and ass. Damn, my girl has a nice ass.

"Did you finish your work for the day?" She asks, out of breath from finishing up a squat.

"No, but I am done for now. Do you want to go exploring?" I give her the smirk I know makes her panties wet. She bites her lip and nods slowly in response. I cross my arms, raise a brow, and look at her through my lashes, shaking my head while laughing under my breath. This is sexual which means she needs to play by the script. She immediately catches on and her eyes find the floor.

"I'm sorry, I meant to say 'yes, mommy'," she corrects herself. I looked around as I was walking up to make sure nobody was close enough to hear our conversation. I wouldn't make her play where others would overhear.

"Let's go, pet." I hold my hand out, waiting for her to take it. I never force anything, she has to be willing. She takes it happily and I lead her to the sauna. Nobody is allowed in there right now due to me cleaning it. But Hasley doesn't know that. When we get there, I grab her a towel from the stand beside the door and lead her inside. Before closing the door behind us, I chain the entrance off and place a sign that states 'temporarily closed for cleaning'. I turn to face her and her eyes darken.

"Take your clothes off," I order. She doesn't hesitate and her eyes don't leave mine. First, she grabs the hem of her navy shirt and pulls it over her head. Her breasts are on full display.

"Where is your bra?" I question her. She shrugs and has an innocent look on her face.

"Oops, must have forgotten it by mistake," she says as she shrugs.

"Take your leggings and panties off and then you will bend over my knee. Coming here braless is getting you spanked," I inform her of her mistake and she bites back a smile.

"What if somebody walks in and sees?" I look at her with irritation because why would I allow somebody else to see what's mine? "Yes, Mommy," she complies. I sit on the ledge of the bench and wait for her. She rushes with excitement and lays over my thighs.

"Tell me why you are in trouble. I want to make sure you understand." Communication is the key to this.

"Because I didn't wear a bra to the gym," she confesses.

"You were taunting everybody around you every time you jumped or ran. They all saw those beautiful tits bounce. They were watching what's mine and I don't appreciate you playing with my head," I say that last thing before I raise my hand and bring it back down making a loud slapping noise on her ass. She lets out a loud moan of enjoyment and I rub the sting out. I repeat the notion four more times before I believe she has learned her lesson.

"Are you going to prance around in public with no bra again?" I quiz leaning over to gauge her emotional reaction while she is still exposed over my lap.

"No, Mommy," she responds and I help her stand up straight. I look her over to get a feel for how her body is responding.

"Are you okay?" I need to make sure that a line wasn't crossed or that she didn't hate it.

"Yes, Mommy. I like it when you punish me," she admits but I don't like the end of what she said.

"Don't turn into a brat. I don't like that. If you ever want to get spanked, just ask," I tell her and then motion for her to sit on the bench. I laid a towel down for her to sit on. It doesn't matter how many times I scrub the seats, it will never be clean. When she gets settled, I sink to my knees between her thighs.

Our eyes are locked when I dive into her sweetness. Her hand rests on the back of my head and she's already moaning. I knew she was going to be ready for me after I punished her. It doesn't take long before she's pushing my face further into her. Her head falls back and her moans are loud. I slip two fingers inside her warmth.

"Fuck yes, Mommy! Fuck me like the bad girl that I am. Yes! Yes! Yes! Right there!" Her words turn into gibberish and her legs start shaking uncontrollably. When her body goes weak, I stand with her ankles in my hand. She looks at me with confusion and I pull her legs to the side so that she is now laying on the bench.

"Oh no, I can't cum again. Let me have a turn," she argues.

"No, you will cum again and you know it," I tell her and then I lie on my stomach and push her legs apart. I let them rest on my shoulders and go back to this swollen pink pussy in my face. She giggles at first but then her hips start grinding on my face. Within minutes she's cumming again, just like I told her she would. After I lick her clean, I help her to her wobbly feet and put her shirt over her head. Her body is shining with sweat. I can feel mine running down my back under my clothes. So maybe the sauna wasn't the best idea, but she seems to feel better.

"Wait, I want to do you." She stops me before I help her into her pants.

"No, I just wanted to make you feel good. You can play with me later in bed, okay?" I compromise while she puts one foot in. It's difficult to pull her pants up because they stick to her legs.

"But Mommy, I want you now," she whines. I look up at her to meet her eyes but she adverts them to the floor beside me.

"Nobody likes to be talked back to. I said no and that's it. If you were to tell me no, I wouldn't say another word about it. It's called respect," I snap at her.

"I'm sorry, Mommy. It won't happen again." She pulls her pants up the rest of the way with a couple of hops. I stand up and kiss her forehead, caressing her cheek with my thumb. She leans into my hand, looks at me, and smiles. With that being settled, I walk out and close the door behind me. I'll take the chain down when I see her leave.

After I finished up with Hasley, I threw myself back into work and the rest of the day went by smoothly. I'm driving home and I know I need to stop and get groceries but I'm worn out. It sounds like a tomorrow plan. I pull up in front of my apartment building and I see Melody's car. *Why don't people call before they show up?*

I'm glad I didn't give anybody a key or they would basically be living here. I grab my phone and wallet and walk up to my door. She's standing there in a black trench coat that stops mid-thigh and six-inch heeled boots that go up to just below her knees. Her red hair looks like it was just washed and straightened. She's wearing bright red lipstick and winged black eyeliner.

"Hello there, can I help you?" I stand a good ten feet away for safety purposes.

"Can we please go inside, Mommy?" She asks while she steps out of the way. I stare at her as I pull my key out and unlock the entrance to my apartment. I open the door and gesture for her to go in first and I follow behind. Damn, she is so sexy.

Once we are deep in the house, she turns to me and takes something out of the coat's pocket. When she places it on her head, I figure it out - black, satin bunny ears. A second later she is untying the coat. She opens it and lets it fall off her arms to the floor.

My heart stops.

She is wearing a sexy bunny costume-black leather, lace sides, corset ties from just below her belly button to her breast. It's not tied tight so I can see most of her skin. Fuck me. It takes a lot for me to exercise patience. I slowly walk to my kitchen counter to place my keys, phone, and wallet down. I'm scared if I move too fast then I will end up holding her with her legs wrapped around me.

"What, um, what are you doing here?" I try to form a question. She puts one foot in front of the other and walks over to me, taking her sweet time.

"I just thought that maybe I could *hop* on over here and play. I wanted to dress up sexy for you. Do you like it?" *What the hell kind of question was that?*

"Do I like it?" I say under my breath. "The only thing that is keeping my mouth off of you is the fucking leather. Tell me, pet. Are you wet for me?" I ask her as I look her over. She slowly gets to her knees and looks at the floor.

"Yes, Mommy," she responds in a soft voice.

"I bought a toy for you the other day, Hasleys won't get here until tomorrow but I can go ahead and play with you. So, do you want to play?" I bought her a neon green dildo that vibrates.

"Yes, Mommy," she says and I help her to her feet.

"Keep your boots and ears on," I command, leading her to my bed. When we get there, I sit on the edge and pull her to straddle me. Her boobs are in my face and damn, it's a fucking sight. Her hands are playing with the back of my hair and mine are on her hips. My teeth are pulling at the strings crossing her breasts and I try to pop it but it's not happening so instead I lick through the holes. She starts moving her hips back and forth, trying to cause friction for herself.

"Keep going and make yourself cum, pet," I whisper and she moves faster and harder. Her head falls to my shoulder and she pulls my hair.

"Fuck, I want to cum. Can I cum Mommy, please?" she moans in my ear. The sound is intoxicating.

"Cum all over me, pet. Cum hard and loud," I tell her through clenched teeth. I move my hand straight to the leather covering one boob, pull the string holding the top together to allow the leather to move easier, and pull it to the side so her nipple is exposed. I bite my bottom lip and wrap my lips around the puckered peak and suck.

"Oh shit. Please bite it, Mommy, please," she begs and of course, I comply. I don't bite down hard but I put enough pressure to turn her moans into enjoyable screams.

"You're such a good fucking pet," I praise when I let her breast go. I put the leather back over that boob and pull the other out. I take hold of that nipple with my teeth and she comes apart.

"Yes, fuck, Mommy. Yes! I'm cumming on you like a good girl," she practically yells in my ear. I stay still until she comes back down to earth. She smiles and starts kissing me, biting my lip and shoving her tongue in my mouth.

"Take that off and lay down on your back," I demand and she does it immediately, keeping her boots and ears on like I told her earlier. Damn, she's amazing. I strip out of my shoes and clothes and get the box from under my bed. I pull out the dildo and show her.

"Would you like to play with this? It's brand new," I ask, wanting her to know that it is all hers. She has a big smile plastered on her face.

"Yes, ma'am," she says with excitement. I crawl on the bed and straddle her stomach, putting the toy at her mouth.

"Suck it." Somehow this turns me on to watch. "That's right, get it nice and wet," I croon.

When she has it slick, I get off her and crawl between her legs. My fingers go straight to her pussy and start playing in her folds. She's still wet from that last orgasm. I push the button and our little neon friend buzzes to life. I slide it back and forth on her clit while my fingers explore her warm entrance, making sure she's wet enough for it.

"You're soaked, pet," I softly moan and she lets out an approval hum. I remove my fingers and replace them with a vibrating toy. I slowly push it inside her, it only takes a few pumps and I watch as her mouth opens wide while her hands are grabbing at the blankets.

"Yes, yes, yes," she pants, and her back arches off the bed. While I'm working her, I slide up to her face and kiss her. She sucks and bites my lip like I'm her personal chew toy.

"Say my name. I want you to cum with it on your lips," I whisper in her ear. She grabs my back and her nails dig in. The sting of the cuts makes me want to ride her face.

"Mommy, fuck me, yes. Make me cum, Mommy!" she screams and her body convulses as she comes apart under me. I pull the toy out, turn it off, and toss it on the floor. *I'll clean it when we are done.* I put my face between her thighs and lick up the evidence of her orgasm.

When I am satisfied, I move up her body and straddle her face. I don't have to say anything, she grabs my thighs and pulls me down so she barely has room to breathe. There's no warning before her tongue starts lapping up my wetness. I was so worked up from fucking her that I'm already on the edge. She starts humming and the vibration sends me over.

"Fuck yes, pet. You're doing such a good job. Right there, yes," I softly moan and start moving my hips without noticing. I grab my breasts and squeeze as my orgasm takes over. I'm not loud like they are when I cum but I make enough noise to where she knows what's happening. I ride it out and her tongue makes its way into my entrance, tasting all of me. I stay still for a moment to get myself together and then move off of her.

Chapter 7

"I need you to write down the things that turns you on and the things I can do when we are playing and you need to be punished," I told Hasley after Clara gives us our coffee. She stops immediately.

"What do you mean by punishment?" She asks, horrified. I need that paper because the way she keeps putting herself down, I have to make her see how beautiful she is.

"Well, that goes with it. It's fun and games but there has to be seriousness in it as well. I will never do anything that you aren't comfortable with and I will take it slow. But I need to know your limits," I explain as I blow on my coffee.

"You're not going to like, hit me with a belt or anything, right?" She sounds scared. We walk up to a small round table by the window and I gesture for her to sit down.

"No, I wouldn't enjoy that at all. There are other things that can be done," I inform her as I take my own seat. "We can talk about everything but I still need them written down. Not because I will forget, I won't, but for safety measures. Maybe you would even want to try something new, something fun." I can see the wheels turning in her head. She takes a sip of her coffee, trying to hide the smile that's only there for a second, but I catch it.

"I'll go online and see what I can find that I want to play around with and I will give you the paper soon. I can't wait to…"

My phone starts ringing and I pull it out of my pocket to look. Melody. It's not weird that she's calling, we talk multiple times throughout the day.

"Hey."

"I need help!"

"Calm down and take a deep breath. What's going on?"

"I really fucked up, Izzy."

"Melody, where are you?"

"I … I took something. Somebody has me. I don't … I don't know where I am."

"Focus, what's around you?"

"It's bright and … NO! Stop, give it back!"

"Melody!"

"She's busy."

The line goes dead. The hair on the back of my neck stands on end. I reach up with my right hand and rub the area to rid myself of the feeling. "Fuck!" I yell out and Hasley is looking at me with concern all over her face.

"What's wrong with Melody?" She puts her hand on my arm as she asks.

"Somebody took her," I tell her plainly but my mind is racing. I leave my coffee on the table and walk out. Hasley is on my heel, panicking.

"What do you mean? Who took her? Where is she? Is she okay?" She spits out question after question. I try not to get annoyed but damn, I don't have any answers. I stop on the sidewalk and turn to face her.

"I don't know. Okay. I don't know anything. Just give me a second to think," I snap at her, feeling bad about it immediately and pull her in for a hug. She's sniffling in my shirt and I am such a fucking mess. "It's okay, I'm sorry about that. I'm just as scared as you are," I soothe her, petting her hair. "Will you stay the night with me? It will make me feel more at ease knowing nobody can get to you," I ask. She nods her head as she wipes her nose. I grab hold of her hand and lead her to my apartment.

Who the fuck would take her and why? She's been clean for years now so I would hope that she stopped hanging out with her old crowd. I never heard her talk about any other friends, hell, I don't think she has even told me about her family. Why did I not care to ask? What the fuck is wrong with me?

The walk home was quiet and Hasley was crying the whole way. We get to my apartment and I let her walk in first.

"Why haven't you called her back? Maybe the person will answer," she points out. I can't believe I didn't think about that. Damn. I kiss her forehead and thank her.

"Go run some bath water, I'll be there in a minute," I tell her so that she doesn't have to listen to this conversation. No need to make her even more upset. When I hear the water, I call Melody's phone. It rings and rings, my nails look like shit now that I've been biting them from anxiety.

"Well hello, Ma'am."

Ma'am... Fuck! My blood runs cold, and chills run down my spine. I know that voice, I know everything there is to know about that voice. I spent 8 months with that voice, I should have recognized it right away.

My body knew it before I did, when she ended the call at Ash's coffee shop. It just didn't register who it actually was until those words. How the fuck did I not put it together? This is the worst possible thing that could have happened today...

"Elise. What the fuck do you think you're you doing?"

"I'm playing. You used to love to play with me, before her."

"You don't know what you're talking about, I didn't leave you for her. I left you months before I even met her."

"Oh, well, she is mine to do whatever with now."

"HELP! Izzy, please!" I hear Melody scream in the background.

"Shut up, bitch." Elise snaps.

I can hear struggling and then Melody starts screaming.

"ELISE! Stop! Shit, just leave her alone."

Melody's still screaming.

"I'm going to have to gag her ... Do you enjoy a little ball gag, cunt?"

"Elise, focus on me. Where are you?"

"I'm at our special spot." Elise pauses before she continues. "Well, I have to go. I want to see how kinky she is. I'm thinking about starting with a little hook suspension. See you around, Ma'am."

I yell her name but it doesn't matter because she has already hung up. Our special spot. We didn't have a spot.

I knew she was fucking crazy but shit. I dial Jace, if he can't help me find her then he can watch Hasley. It only rings twice before he answers.

"Sup, Iz?"

"Fucking Elise took Melody!"

"Shit, where are they?"

"If I knew then I wouldn't be calling you."

"What can I do?"

"Do you remember if I had a special place with her?"

"Damn, well you never told her that you loved her. Y'all fucked everywhere and y'all never were official. Shit, I have no idea."

"Come watch Hasley. That bitch can't take another one of my girls."

"Sure, I'll bring her back to my place."

"Whatever, I don't care."

I hang up on him because I don't have time to talk anymore. I walk to the bathroom and tell Hasley the basics of what's going on before I leave the apartment. I know I should wait for Jace but I can't stand around while Elise is alone with Melody and has all the time in the world to do whatever she is thinking of doing.

Deciding to take my car because the sound of the bike will give me away and I don't know what shape she will be in. When I get in my seat, I check the magazine to my

9mm to make sure she's loaded -all eight- but hopefully it doesn't come to that. I put it back in the console and rack my brain with where she could have taken her. I drive around for half an hour and see nothing.

"FUCK!" I yell out as I hit my steering wheel. She followed me around wherever I went so there was nowhere that I took her for any occasion. I call Melody's phone but it goes straight to voicemail. Shit. Did I keep Elise's number? I look through my contacts and there she is. She answers immediately.

"Yes, ma'am?"

"Where the fuck are you?"

"Hmm, no, I don't want to tell you."

"Elise, stop being a brat."

"You loved it when I acted out."

"That's not me anymore. Where did you take her?"

"Why do you care? You never even checked up on me when we were together."

"Elise."

"What? You couldn't have a real relationship with me but you can with her and that other slut?"

"Don't make this something it's not. Where is she?"

"The other girl was lucky. I went back for her but Jace was driving away before I even parked."

"Where the fuck is she?"

"Nah, I like this game. You are finally giving me the attention I deserve."

"I will find you and when I do... I'm going to fuck you up."

"Oh, Mommy. Talk dirty to me, you know how I like rough play."

I try a different approach because this is going nowhere.

"Pet."
"Yes, Mommy."
"Where are you?"
"At my favorite place."

I think long and hard about when we were fucking. It was only a couple of months ago but I wasn't mentally with her. She was the last sub I had and I'm trying my damnedest not to enter that world again. I can't think of a single fucking place that she could be.

"Pet, I'm growing tired of this game."
"Don't you remember, Mommy? It's where we played for the first time. I think about that night every day. It meant the world to me... You mean the world to me."
"Pet—"

"No! This slut doesn't get to have you! How is she better than me?! What does she have that I don't have?" She doesn't give me any time to respond. **"Hm? Nothing! That's what! If I have my way, you will never see this bitch again, and I will be yours again."** Elise starts talking as if she has pulled the phone away from her ear. **"Hear that bitch? You won't be making it out of here."**

"You touch her and I will never forgive you, Elise. Do you hear me?"

"You're lying."

"Why would I lie about something like that? Can't you see where you have gone so wrong in this? Kidnapping and threatening my girlfriend just because you are jealous."

"I'm not fucking *jealous*!"

"Damn sure sounds like it to me. You can't follow orders, I've asked you multiple times to tell me where the fuck you have taken her. What you have done to her. But all I have gotten is 'I like this game'. This isn't a fucking game anymore, Elise. This is someone's life. My life. Melody's life. Your life. Can't you see that?"

I stepped out of the car, leaving it running just in case she tells me where she is and I can get there quickly. I start to pace around the car, the adrenaline pumping through my veins. I know I won't be able to calm down until I know that Melody is safe. Why the fuck did Elise stay in town? I thought for sure she wouldn't have stuck around after how we left things...

"I don't give a fuck Izzy. It's me or them."

"El—" I don't get to finish her name before I hear the beep beep of the dial tone. "Fuck!" I pull the phone from my ear and check to confirm the line was cut off. I resist the urge to throw my phone to the gravel beneath my feet and instead decide to call the one person I know can calm me down. Hasley. She's probably also freaking out, but hearing her voice right now would help me know that she is safe. So I dial her number.

"Did you find her?"

"No, not yet..."

"Let me help. Please."

"No. You will stay where you are. You can't put yourself at risk. We don't know what she is capable of."

"She? You know who this is?" I can hear Jace and Ash attempting to talk to Hasley, trying to find out what is going on.

"Yes. My ex-girlfriend." I start to cry.

"What would she want with Melody? She hasn't done anything to her. You weren't with her when we started—"

"No! Of course not! We were over months before I met you. Never think that I would do something like that! I have better morals. So please, never think that."

"Okay, just making sure. I still want to help though."

"I don't think it would help, she's got to be inside somewhere, I haven't heard anything when I've called. No wind or birds or people in the background other than Melody. I'm driving around to see if anything sparks a memory or something. So please, I beg you, stay put until I say it's safe. Okay?"

"Okay. I don't like it but I'll stay for now."

"Thank you. I'm going to drive around for a bit longer. I'll talk to you later."

"Bye. Please be safe."

Ending that call was the hardest thing I have had to do all day, but hearing her voice did calm me enough to keep going. I drive around for another couple hours before I am yet again on the side of the road punching my steering wheel. "Fuck, Elise. Where the fuck can you be?" I scream into my hands as a tear slips from the corner of my eye.

My mouth feels like the Sahara desert, I can't get comfortable in my seat as I sink back, dropping my head on the headrest. As my body starts to shake, I attempt to breathe and calm myself but it doesn't work this time. I try to think about something happy but all I can think about are my girls, together, which makes it worse. I have to try and clear my mind entirely. Taking a few moments to get my thoughts and emotions in check, I try one last time, to get Elise to tell me where they are.

"Did you figure it out yet?"

"How can I figure out where you are when you haven't given me any useful hints?"

"I have given you plenty of hints. If you don't know where our special place is, that's not my fault." I had gotten somewhere when I played her game before, maybe it will work again.

"Pet..."

"Yes, Mommy?"

"Tell Mommy where you are," I demand.

"Mommy should already know where I am. Our special place." I hear whimpers come through the phone.

"Pet. Are you crying?"

"No, your little bitch is. Let me just take care of that." The line crackles as if Elise set the phone down and the next thing I hear is her picking the phone back up, **"There. I won't have to listen to her whining anymore. Thank fuck for that."**

"What did you do to her?"

"Nothing, just found some duct tape the other day down here in the basement, so I used that."

"The basement? You mean at your house?"

"Took you long enough, Mommy."

"You will do exactly as I tell you to, right down to the letter."

"We will see about that. Mommy." She enunciates the last word as if she spits it out.

"I want you on your knees, palms up, eyes down before I get there. Do you understand?"

I don't give her time to respond before I hang up. Revving the engine, I take off in the direction I remember her house being. I don't even remember the first time I was with her, I was so drunk at least I'm pretty damn sure I was drunk. I do remember the last time though, clear as day.

Chapter 8

"Look at you, pet. You're so pretty spread out for me on the St. Andrews cross, waiting. What should I do to you? What if I fuck Isabel right here in front of you? Let you get wet enough to drip on the floor. You won't be able to create any friction." She's panting as I wave Isabel over to me.

She starts kissing on my neck while I'm still locking eyes with Elise. Reluctantly I move my eyes away from her and put all of my concentration on making Isabel wet. I nibble her ear, lick along her jaw, and suck on her neck. She lets out breathy moans and I work my way down to her big tits.

They are bigger than my hands and one hundred percent fake. I suck and bite her nipple until they are dark pink and needlepoint. My fingers trail down her side and I grab onto her hips. I throw one of her legs over my shoulder and bury my face in her pussy. Her hands rest on my head for support and she starts moaning.

I hear Elise begging me to touch her but I pay it no mind. She knows how to stop this and that is what I'm listening for. Isabel's legs start shaking and I slide two fingers inside her, making her explode around my fingers. She starts gig-

gling, I pull out and suck her off of my fingers while I look her in the eyes.

"*Flamingo,*" *Elise says and I jump up, unstrap the cuffs on her wrists and then her ankles. She falls in my arms, crying.* "*I can't, I can't do this.*"

"*Shh, it's ok,*" *I soothe her and carry her to the bathroom. I sit her on the toilet and start running the water for a bath. Sticking my hand under the stream coming from the faucet, I check to make sure it's the perfect temperature. I pour in some bubble bath and go get a hair tie off of the sink. Her tears have dried up but around her eyes are pink.*

I pull her hair up in a high bun and kiss her head. She's already talked to me about what not to do during aftercare. Speaking is off the table so I watch her carefully and caress her cheek. When the tub is mostly full, I pick her up and place her in. I start washing her body but she stops me.

"*I can't do this anymore. I don't want to share. Either be happy with only me or leave.*" *She gives me an ultimatum.*

"*I told you from the very beginning that I'm not going to settle down. That's not who I am and I don't want to be that girl. I'm going to make sure you are okay but then I am leaving.*" *I make sure to be very clear. She closes her eyes and takes a deep breath, then blows it out.*

"*I'm not going to be okay. I don't understand why I'm not good enough for you. I can be whatever you want me to be. Please," she pleas and it is sad but I'm not going to be unhappy. That leads to more problems than just heartbreak.*

"You're going to be okay. It might be upsetting right now but you will move on and somebody is going to give you all their time and you're going to be so happy. You will be okay." I try to help her see the positive in this without spitting out shit that's a lie. I want to leave but I'm not going to bullshit my way through this. "I'm going to wash your hair. Look up." I get the black cup off of the side of the tub and fill it with water. She still lets tears fall as I pour the water down her blonde hair. I squeeze the bottle of Tea Tree shampoo in my hand, then lather it in her hair. When I feel like I have gotten all of it, I get the same black cup and wash the soap out.

"I don't want your hands on my body. You can go, take the other girl with you. Bye," she dismisses me but doesn't look up.

I'm so caught up in the memory that I almost passed her house. It's a three-story brick home with a big ass pool out back. It's fancy as hell, even the fucking mailbox is nice -it's a mini house-. It's not money she's earned, oh no, mommy and daddy give her a shit load every month and she doesn't have to do anything for it.

Must be nice. I park on the side of the road and pull my gun out to check that the safety is on. Taking a deep breath, I get out of my car and slide it into the back of my pants. I don't want to use it but I will shoot the bitch if needed.

Not even a second thought.

Before I head inside I send Hasley a text.

> **ME: Elise took Melody to her house. Going there now.**
>
> **Hasley: Send me the address, and I'll meet you there.**
>
> **ME: No, it is too dangerous. I'll let you know.**
>
> **Hasley: Just get our girl back safely.**
>
> **ME: That's my goal.**

Returning the phone to my pocket, I take the front steps two at a time. Getting to the door, I shake the nerves out of my arms and try to turn the handle. It twists, I push the door open, close it behind me, and go to the basement. A million images run through my head before I get to the bottom.

She better not have fucking hurt her. I step on the gray concrete floor, taking one last breath before seeing if she complied with my order, I turn to face the rest of the room, walking around the stairs to take in every corner.

Elise is doing exactly what I said. On her knees, palms up, eyes down. She visibly stiffens when my steps get closer. I look up from her to find Melody on her stomach with her upper arms, mid-arm, and wrist bound to her ankles. She's passed out with a cut cheekbone and blood leaking out of her mouth. I run to her and drop to my knees.

"Melody, baby. Come on. Wake up." I check her pulse and I feel the rhythmic beat. It's strong and steady. Good. I try to untie the knots but the rope is too tight for me to undo and I see cut marks on her pants. I stand and take the two steps to Elise.

Crouching down in front of her, I give her the calmest command I can muster right now, "Give. Me. The knife." But she doesn't move. She was always a brat and tested my patience. I don't have time for her shit, I pull my gun out and push the barrel to her forehead. "Give me the God-damn knife Elise or I will put a bullet through your fucking head. Don't fucking try me." She looks up and her eyes meet mine.

"Do it," she calls my bluff.

"You are playing a dangerous game. She is one of the loves of my life and I will not hesitate to fucking end you," I admit to her and myself. Yes, I fucking love Melody and Hasley. I didn't think I would ever have this but I do, I have it now and I'm sure as shit not going to let anybody get in my way. She just stares up at me, silent.

Fuck, can I do this?

Nope.

I lower my gun and walk around to look for something to cut the ropes. I'm fumbling through papers, a cup, and pencils laying around on a metal work table. Anger takes hold of me and I swipe everything off to the floor with my free hand. "Ahh!" I yell out ready to bolt upstairs to the kitchen for a knife but then I hear a clang to my left and rush to it. A pocket knife fell to the floor with all the papers.

"Yes!" I rush to Melody, place my gun on the floor beside me, and start cutting the bondage. My hands are slippery with sweat and the knife slips and cuts a finger on my other hand. "Fuck," I say under my breath but I don't stop until the only parts of her that are still together are her ankles. I almost forget that Elise is here... almost. Giggling brings me back to the present.

"It's cute that you think she'll want you after all this. Do you think this will all go away and she will forget?" Elise asks but I try to ignore her taunts. My focus stays on the tan rope I'm sawing through. Sweat is running down my face but I won't stop until Melody is free. At the same time as I cut through the last threads, I toss the knife to the other side of Melody, far from anyone's easy reach and take her head in my hands.

Frantically I wipe her strawberry hair out of her eyes and kiss her forehead. "She doesn't want you anymore. I told her about how she is being used and that you will toss her away just like you did me. She told me how you would come and save her but I informed her of how wrong she was. Delusional," she is still talking and pushing me to my limit.

I'm fucking done.

I pick my gun up, twist my body around, and shoot. That shuts her up. It takes me a minute for my brain to catch up to what I just did. I'm not sure what I had hit, but I know I hit something, I heard her scream and the thud of her hitting the floor...

"Shit," is all I say, but then everything rushes back into place, and the severity of what I have done. I drop the gun, pull my phone out, and call the cops. While it rings, I place a long kiss on Melody's head. "It's okay, baby. I got you, it will be okay." Everything seems to slow down for a minute and I just watch the blood start to pool under Elise's body.

"9-1-1, what's your emergency?" The lady on the other end says and everything hits fast forward.

"Yeah, umm, my girlfriend was kidnapped and I shot somebody..." it spills out of my mouth so fast.

"Ma'am, calm down and slowly tell me what's going on," she tries again.

"I shot somebody." *Why am I telling her this? Fuck, because I'm a good fucking person and I can't leave her here to bleed out.*

"Where are you?" She asks calmly and I hear the tapping of the keyboard she's using.

"Umm, shit. Sorry, it's 582 Burlin road. We're in the basement," I tell her but then my focus goes back to Melody. "I need help. My girlfriend was kidnapped and she needs an ambulance."

"Ma'am, are you hurt?" She asks, still typing.

"No. Please help my girlfriend!" I unintentionally yell at her.

"The police and ambulance are en route. The person that was shot, are they breathing?" I stare at Elise but I don't move from Melody.

"I don't know. I have my girlfriend and I'm not leaving her," I respond honestly.

"Is your girlfriend stable?" She asks and I already know what's coming.

"She's breathing," I breathe, looking down at Melody.

"You need to check on the other person." I look back and forth between them and take the phone off of my ear for a minute to think. I gently lay Melody's head on the floor.

"I'll be right back, baby," I tell her even though I know she can't hear me. Reluctantly I stand and walk over to Elise. I push her to her back with my foot. I'm not going to be gentle with her, she's lost my respect. I stare at her chest and it's rising and falling, she's breathing hard, and groaning, unable to keep her eyes open. I run my gaze down her body and see the blood where her ribs end.

"She's alive," I state to the person on the other end. I spend no more time watching her and go back to my girl. I sit on the floor and pull her onto my lap.

"Where did you shoot her?"

"Under the ribs," I respond in a monotone because I really don't care what happens to her.

"You need to apply pressure to slow the bleeding. The ambulance will be there in seven minutes," she informs me but I don't move. "Ma'am, keep talking to me until they get there."

"Okay, my girlfriend is still out but she is still breathing," I tell her as I watch Melody's chest rise and fall.

"Has the bleeding from the other girl slowed any?" She drags my attention from Melody to Elise.

"No, it's the same as it was." I'm not lying, but I'm not going to tell her that I haven't tried to stop it either.

"Put more pressure and hopefully it will slow down," she says and I still don't move.

The sirens are quiet at first but then get louder as the team gets closer. It seems like seconds later and I hear footsteps running above me. People come down the stairs fast and take in the scene in front of them. One paramedic goes to Elise and one runs over to me.

"I'm Kyle, what's your name?" The guy with short black hair, green eyes, and tattoos all over his tan arms asks.

"Izzy, this is my girlfriend, Melody," I tell him quickly. He pulls out his stethoscope and listens to her heart while asking me a line of questions.

"Can you tell me what happened here?"

"Yeah, umm, so my ex over there drugged Melody and took her. When I found them, she had Melody tied up and unconscious," I say in one long breath.

"What did she take?" He asks as he counts her pulse.

"I don't know. She called me scared several hours ago." I'm trying to hold back tears but it's no use.

"Is she allergic to anything?" I realize that I don't know the basic things that I should.

"I don't know," I reply softly.

"Does she have family around?" He asks another basic question and it pisses me off.

"I don't know! Okay! Just make her better," I yell out.

"I will do the best that I can. I'm going to give her a shot of Narcan. It overrides most drugs she could have taken." He says as he walks off. Then the two police officers walk up to me.

"Can we ask you a few questions?" The male officer asks.

"I guess I can't say no," I respond a bit snarky. Kyle comes back and gives Melody a shot in her thigh. He holds her wrist to keep up with her pulse and stares at her. Melody starts grunting and she slowly opens her eyes. I start kissing the top of her head, her forehead, and her cheek. "Thank God! Baby, I'm so sorry," I tell her as I cry a river. She's okay. She's okay.

"Ma'am, can you tell me your name?" Kyle asks her and I shoot him daggers. I fucking have her and I don't need his help.

"Melody," she answers him.

"What is the date today?" He asks another fucking question.

"Wednesday," she answers him again.

"Does anything hurt?" She takes a minute to think about his question and then she starts holding her wrists.

"My wrists and ankles hurt. I have a headache and I feel sick." She gives him the list of injuries.

"I need to take you to the hospital to get looked at. Do you remember what medication you took?" He asks and her eyes go wide. She starts crying and covers her face.

"Oxys. I fucking took an Oxy! I can't believe I did that! I was clean for five years! FIVE YEARS! All of that down the drain. I'm so fucking stupid. I worked so hard to be good," she trails off and I have to hold her face in my hands and pull her to look me in the eyes.

"You listen to me. You are not stupid. You are amazing, kind, good, and loving. It was one weak moment. It happens to all of us." Out of the corner of my eye, I see two paramedics lifting Elise onto a stretcher and rolling her to the ambulance that I did not hear pull up. "Don't ever think anything bad about yourself. I am here to help you get through this and I'm not leaving. Do you understand me? You are strong and this will not define you," I tell her as tears pour out of her eyes. The paramedic walks up to us with a stretcher and interrupts our heart-to-heart. *What the fuck, man?*

"We really need to get you to the hospital to get checked out," Fucking Kyle says. The police officer clears her throat.

"Ma'am, can we have a few minutes of your time?" She gestures to the other side of the room where we would be out of the way for the paramedics.

I feel my aggravation rise and all I want to do is punch her in the face. I smile and say, "Of course. What can I do for you?" In my best customer service voice. The only way I am getting through any of this without being directly beside Melody.

"Alright, Miss...?" she starts.

"Miss Matthews"

"Thank you Miss Matthews. We will just get started, it shouldn't take very long. Can you tell us what happened, from the beginning?" I try my best to resist the urge to roll my eyes. *Why do I have to repeat this? I already told the dispatcher what happened...* But I start my explanation from the first time Melody called me.

"Why didn't you call the police when you got off the phone the first time?" W*hat kind of fucking question is that?*

"I don't know. I just figured you guys wouldn't have done anything because it had only been a few hours and not over twenty-four like I've heard about kidnappings and police involvement." My foot starts to involuntarily tapping on the ground and I recognize that my arms have crossed, closing myself off to the lady cop. I need to get back to Melody, she really needs to stop talking.

"What is your relation to the gunshot victim?" This bitch is really getting on my nerves with all the questions. I thought this was going to be quick.

"Elise is my ex-girlfriend and she got super jealous that I moved on and she didn't. That is my best guess as to why she did this. That's your next question. Right?" I can feel the attitude slipping into my responses and I try to pull back but the words just keep flowing, question after question. If she was phased by my response she never showed it. I understand she sees this type of situation on the regular but still she has to realize that my brain isn't in these questions, it's with my girlfriend getting poked and prodded across the room. I allow her voice to fade into the background while I stare at Melody.

I can see that she is more alert and talking better than when she woke up. I notice her try and sit up but the paramedics stop her before she even gets her head off the pillow. *Assholes. She should be able to sit up if she wants to...*

"Ma'am, are you listening?" I am whipped back into reality by the lady cops voice. It's so fucking annoying and high pitch. She seems too perky for her job.

"I'm sorry I am not here mentally. I haven't processed what happened yet and I think it is just starting to hit me of what I did." It's not a lie, but also not the complete truth.

"That's no problem. Shooting someone takes a while to process the first time it happens, especially if it is in self-defense like in your situation." I am shocked by what she says. I for sure thought that this woman was about to arrest me for shooting Elise and not helping her.

"I'm sorry." I shake my head to clear it. "Can you say that again?"

"Pardon Ma'am?"

"I'm not going to jail?" I couldn't have heard her correctly...

"Yes, Ma'am. From what you and the victim—"

"Melody," I cut in, she is no victim and I will not have them calling her one. She is my girlfriend, a human being and they should treat her like one.

"—Melody. I apologize, Ma'am. From what you and Melody have said about the situation, everything was self-defense. You will not be going to jail, just don't go around shooting anyone else with that gun or we will be taking it and using it to cross-examine against other unsolved cases." She's joking, the bitch has humor. Fuck that actually makes me like her just a bit. If I didn't have my girls, I probably would have tried to get her into bed tonight.

She asks many questions about what Elise said, how I found them, and what I did when I arrived. Step by step. It annoyed the fuck out of me.

"Last question, Miss Matthews. Has either of these women shown signs of knowing each other before today?" *What the fuck?*

"No, I haven't spoken to Elise in months. The only people who knew each other here was through me, they didn't know each other and I sure as hell didn't introduce them. Are we done here?"

"I apologize for sounding insensitive Ma'am, it was just a question. That is all for now, please stick close by just in case we have more questions for you later." I nod to her and say nothing else as she walks up to her partner to compare notes about what was said.

I follow Melody into the ambulance and sit on the blue leather seat beside her, buckle myself up, and reach out to hold her hand. They have her strapped down with orange buckles in three spots over her legs and two crossed over her chest. For the first time since she woke up, I look her over. She's shivering but sweat is trailing down her forehead. I'm about to ask her how she feels when she turns her head away from me and pukes. Shit. I gather her hair and pull it out of her way.

"Why is she throwing up? What did you do to her?" I don't take my eyes off Melody as I bark out questions to Kyle.

"She's okay, just coming off of the narcotics that she took. Her body is going through withdrawal." He calmly tells me. I am anything but calm.

"What can I do? Just tell me and I'll do it," I cry out to Melody. She just shakes her head and holds up a finger to tell me to wait. Kyle pulls out a napkin and I snatch it out of his hands. I don't fucking like him and he doesn't need to take care of her. She's my fucking girl and I can handle it.

"Turn your head and look at me, baby," I say to her but she doesn't move. "Look at me, pet. I won't say it again." She complies and I don't miss the look that Kyle gives me. This life isn't for everybody and the people that don't really know shit, make it very obvious. Melody looks up at me and tears are running from her glassy eyes. "Shh, it's okay. Let me take care of you." I gently wipe her tears away and then her mouth.

After her face is cleaned up, I toss the dirty rag at the paramedic's face. He quickly swipes it off him and gives me this eat-shit look but is smart enough not to say anything. I go back to holding Melody's hand, trying to steady her tremors. "It's okay, I'm here. I'm here and I am not fucking leaving you." She doesn't say anything but words aren't needed

We arrive at the hospital and rush out of the ambulance, and into the building. Once through the doors, we are met by two female nurses. The paramedic tells the nurses what happened, what they gave her, her heart rate, and other things that I pay no attention to. I haven't let go of Melody's hand since the ambulance and I don't plan to. She is still shaking and her eyes are screwed shut.

"It's okay, I'm here. You're doing great. I am so proud of you," I try to calm her.

"You can sit in the waiting room while we get her checked out," one of the nurses tells me, pointing to an area with blue plastic-like chairs.

"Yeah, fuck that. I'm not leaving her," I tell her while giving her a 'fuck you' look.

"Are you her sister?" The nurse asks, looking me up and down.

"No, I try not to fuck family," I deadpan. That takes her back and starts apologizing.

"I want... I want her... to stay... with me," Melody says between her teeth chattering. That seems to be enough because we all head for a room in the ER. It's a basic area with a shitty bed, shitty walls, and a shitty tv. There's a sink on one side of the room, a ventilator at the head of the bed, and a monitor on the other side.

I don't let her go as they velcro the cuff on her upper arm and the pulse oximeter on her finger. She lets go of my hand when the cuff turns on but I don't leave, I just lay my hand on her wrist. I almost forgot about the markings there. Images of her tied up run through my mind and I'm pissed again.

"She's fine!! Can you put something on the rope burns instead of checking to see if she's breathing? It's obvious that she is!" I snap at the nurse.

"Izzy, it's okay. Don't... don't yell at her." Her eyes pleaded with me. Fine, but I'm not fucking apologizing. The nurse stares at me while putting a metal pan in Melody's lap.

"Okay, just hold your arms over the pan and I'm going to pour some cold, sterilized water over it. This will wash off all of the debris and fragments from the rope." She educates Melody in a soft, caring voice. She proceeds to slowly pour the water and Melody flinches.

"What's wrong?" I ask her.

"It just stings. I'm fine." Her shaking is slowly stopping and her teeth are no longer clattering. The nurse does the same thing with Melody's ankles. It's hard to watch but I don't avert my eyes. I deserve this. She is here because of me. If I didn't allow a fucking crazy bitch in my life then we would be at home with Hasley. Oh shit! Hasley. I pull my phone out quickly and dial her number. It doesn't ring. I look down at the screen and of course, no signal. Fucking hospitals…

"It's okay, go call her. She has to be freaking out." Melody tells me when she notices my problem.

"Are you sure? I don't want to just leave you," I ask her just in case. She just smiles up at me and nods. I kiss her forehead and reluctantly walk away. I run through the halls to get out of the building. People are staring at me and whispering. Luckily I don't give a fuck right now. When I get outside there are sirens and people yelling. I'm not walking any further from Melody so this will have to do.

I check the signal, finally, and dial Hasley's number again.

"Finally! Is she okay?"

"Yes, she is okay. Just a little shaken up and some rope burns."

"Good. I've been over here pacing, waiting for you to call. You sure took your sweet time."

"I'll let that one slide, pet."

"THIS ISN'T THE TIME, MOMMY. WE AREN'T FUCKING!" I hear the sarcasm in her voice but I pay it no attention, I have too much on my mind to think about disciplining her.

"Maybe not right now but it will bite you in the ass later. I have to get back to her but I will call you when they discharge her."

"No. What hospital are you guys at? I'm coming to you. I need to see that she is alright with my own eyes."

"Pet, no. You don't want to see her this way. We will be out of here in no time. I will call you, I promise, if anything changes and you can come then to wait. But for now, you would be doing the same thing as you are right now, just in a hard as fuck chair. Be comfy, take a bubble bath, and read a book. Do something to take your mind off what is happening right now. Okay?"

"I'm sorry. Okay, I will be waiting. Don't forget about me, please." I hear the deflated tone come from her and it breaks my heart. I almost open my mouth to tell her to come here and we can wait together, but I know for right now, she is better off at home. With Jace and Ash, where someone can keep an eye on her. I know that Elise is somewhere in this hospital and can't hurt her but I still like knowing she's safe.

I hang up and pocket my phone. I rush back to Melody and just as I'm walking in, a man walks out.

"Who the fuck was that?" I ask, furious.

"Doctor Sullivan. He said that everything looks good but they want to keep me here for another hour." She tells me. I grab her hand and pull it to my lips for a kiss.

"How are you feeling?" I know she has to be tired of that question by now, but I can't help to ask it anyway.

"I can't believe I did that. I was doing so good and just like that, boom, five years down

the fucking drain." She is still beating herself up.

"We are going to get through this. Hasley will be there too. You are not going to do this alone." I promise her.

"It's just crazy that your ex was there, watching me. Was she always that crazy?" She brings up a sore point for me.

"No, she used to be very easygoing. I actually had no idea she was still in town." I think back to how Melody is here because of that psycho.

"What happened with you and her?" She pushes and has every right to know.

"She wanted me to herself and I couldn't do that. I was very clear about my taste when we got together." I spill everything to her. Her eyes are filled with pity and that isn't what I want at all. If anything, I should be the one feeling shitty. I drop her hand and look away. "I have to go ask the nurse a question, I'll be right back." I take a deep breath and walk out of the room. The nurse's station is right around the corner and I stop to talk to them.

"Hey, there was a girl that got here over an hour ago in an ambulance, where is she?" I ask them and one speaks up.

"What's her name?" She asks me.

"Elise Warring." I can't believe I remember her last name. She only told me once at the beginning of whatever the fuck we were doing. The nurse looks at her computer and finds her after a minute.

"She's in emergency surgery..."

Chapter 9

"Surgery?" I asked again.

"The doctor will be out soon to talk with you." The nurse doesn't take the sorry look off her face. I shot her but made sure it wasn't at any serious spots. What did I do? Fuck! I stumble back and mindlessly walk to the waiting area. I'm so lost in thought, I almost didn't hear my phone ringing. Of course the only spot in the hospital that gets service is the waiting room… It's Jace, probably just to check-in.

"Hello."

"Hey Iz, what's going on?"

"Melody is fine but Elise is in emergency surgery."

"Iz, it's just me. What happened?"

"I shot her but I made sure it was low and wouldn't do any serious damage."

"Apparently it wasn't too clear of a shot."

"I'm freaking out. What if I killed her, Jace? What am I going to do? What will Melody and Hasley think of me?"

"They are going to think about how you rescued and saved Melody. They're going to think that you put them before yourself."

"I just... I don't know."

"I'm coming to you. What hospital? Room number? You know you can't do this alone Iz, let us be there for you." A tear rolls down my cheek, my heart feels so full I can barely stand it. I never thought I would have friends like this. I never thought I would have a family like this. Every single one of them is someone I would die for. I can't see my life without any of them.

I hear Hasley yelling in the background... "You better not leave me! I'm going with you and you can't stop me!"

"Hasley will be there too."

I tell him where I am and hang my phone up. With my elbows on my knees and my head in my hands, I cry. I let it all out. It's too much. Hasley, Melody, Elise. I cry and cry some more.

I've never felt this worthless. After a few minutes, I sniffle up all the nasty shit running out of my nose, wiped my eyes, and stood up. *Get your shit together!* I fan my face while walking back to Melody.

When I get there, she is asleep. I walk over to the chair beside the bed and sit, trying not to wake her. She's had a shit day. Fuck.

I can't get over this nagging thought though. I don't ever want her to have to go through this again. What if Elise comes out of this and wants to try and fuck this up again? What if next time she does serious damage? I can't let that happen. I have to protect her.

There's a knock at the door and I jump up but then Jace walks in with Hasley and I sink back into my chair. Hasley pushes Jace out of the way and runs to me. I pull her onto my lap but she doesn't sit all the way down.

"I swear, Hasley. Don't make me mad." That's all I had to say and she sits fully. "You aren't going to break me. I love every curve," I say in more of a growl and kiss her shoulder.

"How is she doing?" Jace asks me. All three of us look over at Melody but I know he isn't asking about her. He already knows she is good. I shake my head slightly, not wanting Hasley to notice.

"Melody is resting but she will be able to leave soon. Once they feel comfortable with her stability," I tell them both. "How is Ash feeling?"

"She is very confused right now. She cries and laughs at the same time. I don't even know. She came with us, just getting you some food and coffee from the Starbucks down the road. I told her that you don't eat when you are stressed but she insisted. Just take it and like it. I swear, if you tell her no she will go crazy." Jace looks so serious when he tells me that and I almost laugh.

"Jace, are you scared of your fiancée?" I ask him and I don't hold back the smile.

He stands a little straighter and points his finger at me.

"Don't you dare judge me. She was already scary but now she's even worse," he shuts up and takes a step back when the door opens. Ash is walking in with two coffees and a little bag.

"Awe, babe. You didn't have to get me coffee." Jace smiles sweetly at Ash. She rolls her eyes when she passes him and walks to me.

"Don't worry, I didn't. You can get your own fucking drink," Ash tells him and hands me mine. "Here, Izzy. It's a white chocolate mocha. That is your favorite, right?" she asks me with a questionable face. Even if it weren't, I would drink it with a fucking smile.

"Yes, thank you so much." And put the cup to my lips. I can feel the heat from the liquid touch me before the actual coffee does. It's hot enough to burn but I don't dare flinch.

"Mmm, this is so good," I say to nobody in particular. She gives Hasley hers and she takes it a little more excited than necessary.

"I also brought you some egg bites with bacon bites. I assume you haven't eaten." Ash watches me intently. I take the bag from her and pop one in my mouth. They are so fucking hot too.

I try to talk with a mouth full. "Thank you so much. It's delicious." I suck in air to hopefully cool my mouth off a little. Ash seems happy enough and stands by Jace. I watch him try to put his arm around her but she slaps him off.

"You're doing it again," Jace whispers to Ash. She doesn't even look at him when she responds.

"Go fuck yourself."

"Okay then," Jace says in defeat. Poor guy. I know they are happy together because Jace tells me all about their personal life.

"I think I'm going to check to see if Elise is out of surgery," I tell the group and try to help Hasley off of me but she gives me this look that I don't understand. Pissed, maybe?

"What do you care if she is or not?" Hasley asks me, accusingly.

"I shot her, Hasley. I need to make sure she is okay," I respond to her but her facial expression isn't changing.

"She took Melody from us! She deserves whatever she gets," Hasley almost yells. I grab her hand and pull her up so that I can stand.

"I'll be right back. Stay here, please," I demand but in a sweet way so that maybe she will listen and do as she's told. I turn and walk past Jace, giving him a look that tells him to watch her. We have been friends for so long that I don't need to use words for him to get it.

When I am in the hallway, I stop and lean against the wall. *Just breathe, it will be okay.* I gather myself and go to the nurse's station again.

"Hey, I was told that the doctor was going to see me about Elise but nobody came. Are there any updates?" I ask the same nurse that I talked to last time. She types away on her computer and her face drops.

"She is still in surgery, I'm sorry but I don't have any other information," she informs me.

"It was just a bullet wound. How long does it take to pull it out and patch her up?" I ask frantically.

"I'm very sorry but I don't have anything more to tell you." I know she has something. She's holding back, but why not tell me? Fuck. I slap my hand on the counter and everybody looks over at me. I just shake my head and go back to the room with Melody. Everybody stares at me as I walk in but when I look at Hasley, I get chills. She looks so fucking mad. What did I miss? I slowly walk into the room.

"Did you get everything you wanted?" Hasley asks me. *Fuck, why is she always so jealous?*

"There's no update, she's still in surgery," I tell everybody but I don't look away from Hasley's stare.

"Oh darn," Hasley says in a smart-ass tone and rolls her eyes.

"Hasley, I think that's enough. It doesn't matter what she did, nobody deserves to die. Especially by my hand." I tell her but she's not having it. She stands quickly.

"Then why take the damn gun with you if you didn't want to hurt the poor baby?" She asks me.

"I took it just in case I needed to distract or wound her. But it was never my intention to cause serious damage." I'm very stern with her at this point. I understand her irritation with Elise but she is being too much. "Watch your next words very carefully, you don't want to say something out of the way and regret it later." She looks away from me and sits back down in her seat. I can hear her huffing and puffing from here. If I had her in the fucking bedroom right now, I would spank the sass right out.

You know what, nope. I will do this in front of everybody.

I walk up to Hasley and grip her neck, her eyes look up to mine. "Keep up your shit and I will handle you appropriately." I watch her movements to make sure that she isn't uncomfortable. "Do you understand?"

"Yes." She bites out. I don't look away but I clench my teeth.

"Excuse me?" I snap because she is being a fucking brat.

"Yes, mommy." She tries again. I hold her gaze for a minute longer and then let my hand drop. I look over at Jace and Ash, they are not even trying to hide the expression on their faces. I know I'm going to get a slew of questions when everything settles down and we are at home. I tell Jace everything but he doesn't know about my dominance in the bedroom, he just knows that I like sex a lot.

This just opened up a whole can of worms. I ignore their questioning gaze and walk over to Melody, grabbing her hand and her eyes start fluttering. They open and she starts smiling.

"You're still here," Melody says to me in surprise. I scrunch up my eyebrows in confusion.

"Did you think I was going to leave you here? No, I'm here," I tell her and make sure she really hears me. "When this is all over, the three of us are going to go on a trip. I promise." Hasley comes up beside me and hops on the bed with Melody.

"Thank God you are okay! I was so worried, don't you ever try and leave me again." Hasley cries in Melody's chest. Melody pets Hasley's hair and tries to soothe her.

"It's okay, babe. I'm okay." Melody says over and over. Jace walks up to us with Ash behind him.

"Hello, Melody. It's nice to finally meet you. Wish we could have met before this." He says to her and it hits me that none of them have met.

"Oh shit, I'm so sorry. Fuck. Melody, Hasley, this is my best friend Jace, and his fiancée, Ash. Jace, Ash, these are my girlfriends, Melody and Hasley." I give formal introductions that are seriously overdue.

"We kind of already met when he picked me up from your house, but it's nice to meet y'all anyways," Hasley says.

"It's nice to meet you both. Thank you for looking out for me, I appreciate it." Melody tells them.

"It's nice to finally meet the people who have made this lady finally settle down," Jace says with a big-ass smile. Ash is staying behind Jace but I can see the tears falling from her eyes and I give Jace a questioning look. He just shakes his head so I will have to remember to ask him about it later.

"Melody, I'll be right back," I tell her and step past Jace, walking to the door. Elise is still in my brain even though she shouldn't be. It's not that I don't care about her, I will always have a soft spot for her. I mean we have a history that can't be erased.

But then again, she did take my girl away from me and put her through hell. I don't want to ask Melody what happened in that basement just yet but I need to know. I have to know what was done to her because of me. I need to feel that pain.

I make my way back to the nurse's desk and I don't have to say anything this time. She types something on her computer and tells me that Elise is out of surgery and she will tell the doctor that I'm out here waiting for an update. So I sit my ass down in one of the chairs and wait. It doesn't take long before a tall man with a white coat walks up to me.

"Are you Ms. Warring's family?" He asks me. I go to say that I'm not but then he won't tell me anything, so I lie.

"I'm her sister. What's going on?" I ask him and he looks me straight in the eye.

"She came in with a bullet wound in her sternum and had to go into emergency surgery. I got the bullet out but she did lose a lot of blood. She is in the recovery room and still heavily sedated." He didn't say she died. I drop to my knees crying because I'm so fucking happy right now. The doctor lets me have my moment but once I stand up and ask to see her, he shoots me down.

"But I want to see her! What can't I go in there?" I'm practically yelling at him now.

"She is still being looked after and she needs to rest," he tells me in such a calm voice that I get pissed off even more. Somebody grabs my upper arm and pulls me, I turn to them but see that it's just Jace. I didn't hear him walk up but I crash into his chest and cry.

"Thank you, doctor," Jace says to him and I'm going to assume that the man leaves.

Chapter 10

Melody is getting discharged and the nurse hands her pamphlets with the letters 'NA' on them. What is that? I take one from her to read the paper. Narcotics Anonymous. Wait...

"She doesn't have a fucking problem, she doesn't need this. It was one slip up and won't happen again." I snap at the nurse.

"When somebody comes in here with medication in their system, we have to provide help." The nurse says back. Melody grabs my hand and pulls me to her.

"It's okay. I want to do this, I need to," Melody says to me with pleading eyes to leave the lady alone. Fine. I gather all the paperwork and help Melody out of the room. We pass the nurse's station and give them instructions to call me with any updates. Getting to my car, I help Melody in and buckle her. I walk around to the other side and open the door for Hasley. Before she gets in, I grab the back of her neck and pull her in for a rough, owning kiss.

"Have I ever given you a reason to question my loyalty?" I ask her. She shakes her head fast.

"No, ma'am." She responds with flushed cheeks.

"Don't ever question it again." I let her go and she sits down. Just like Melody, I buckle Hasley in.

The traffic isn't bad so we get to my house with ease and I carry Melody to my apartment and sit her down on the couch.

"How are you feeling?" I ask her while I pour her a glass of water.

"I'm fine, really. You don't have to baby me." She giggles. I want to tell her that it's not me babying her, this is me loving her. But I bite my tongue because I don't know if I can stay with them. If being with me is going to put them in danger, it's not worth it. It will kill me but their safety is more important.

I hurry to my room and change clothes. I slide on my leather pants with zip pockets, a white tank top, and my leather jacket that has zipper pockets on the chest and on either side. Checking myself out in the mirror, I notice how sad I look. Whatever, time to go.

"I have something that I need to take care of. Will y'all be okay here for a couple hours?" I ask them, I need the space to get my thoughts straight.

"Yes, ma'am. I will look after her and give her anything she needs to help her relax," Hasley says and gives Melody a wink. I give them a smile and get my keys and helmet.

I like being on my bike. It helps me think and relax at the same time. I put my hair in a fishtail braid before I put my helmet on. I don't feel like sitting forever to get the knots out of it when I get back.

I start the motorcycle and listen to the rumble of the motor, feel the vibrations on my thighs, the heat on my lower legs—even with my skinny leather pants. It is so good that I get chills. My baby always makes me feel better and I haven't even hit the road yet.

I put on my GDM Ghost helmet and connect my phone to it. This is the best thing I've purchased to go with my bike. I normally put my phone on do not disturb and crank the music up. I find my driving playlist, press play, and secure it in the chest pocket.

The music starts playing... *I have this thing when I get older, but just never wiser...* Oh, Taylor. I push back the kickstand with my foot and ease out of my parking spot. I pull into the road and give it some gas. I don't know where I'm going but I need to figure my shit out.

I don't get very far before I see Ms. Beth sitting on the sidewalk in front of the ice cream shop, Sweet Snowballs. I slow to a stop in front of her, turn my bike off and pull the kickstand out with my foot. I hop off and take my helmet off.

"Well, aren't you just sex on a bike?" Ms. Beth says. This lady does not talk her age.

"I was hoping I could get you wet," I say back and she smiles. "What are you doing sitting out here?"

"You just said it. I'm sitting here, what more do you want?" She looks at me like I'm the stupid one.

"Can I talk to you about something?" Jace has always talked about how she gave him the best advice so maybe she can help me.

"You sure can. I don't have anywhere to be." She expands her arms like nothing is going on around us. So I sit down on the sidewalk beside her.

"I'm seeing two girls right now and it's great but something happened. One of my exes made an introduction and it really hurt one of my girls. The problem has been worked out but I can't help but blame myself for all of this. She wouldn't have gotten hurt if I didn't mess around with that crazy bitch." Fuck, I didn't mean to cuss at her. "I'm sorry, I didn't mean to say that." She swats at me before I can finish apologizing.

"Fuck that cunt." She says and I stare at her in shock. What the fuck just came out of her mouth? "That's right, I said fuck her. Are your ladies okay?"

"It was only one but she's fine. She is actually a lot better than I thought she would be." I admit.

"Does she blame you or is she mad?" I know where these questions are leading.

"No, but I still hate myself for this. They deserve so much better." I try not to cry while I spill my heart to her.

"Shut the hell up and get over yourself. If they don't want you then they will leave. I already know who you are with. This is a small town and word travels fast. I have talked to Hasley at a time or two. And with Melody being my granddaughter, I seem to know her too." *What the hell?*

"She's your granddaughter? Oh my God, Ms. Beth. I had no idea." I am telling her all of this shit and she's kin to her? Damn.

"She's no saint, darling. I already knew that. We don't talk about her personal life and I would like to keep it that way. But the point in saying that is that I know Melody and if she doesn't want to be somewhere or with someone, she won't," she tells me what I already know but I just didn't want to acknowledge it.

"I guess you're right," I say under my breath but she hears me.

"Well obviously. I'm always right." She has a smug grin.

"It's crazy how your hearing aids are working now but they don't work when I call you." I give her a questioning look that says 'I know what you're up to'.

"Oh, sweetheart, that's called selective hearing. Go. Finish your drive and get back to your ladies." She orders but then she looks uncomfortable.

"You're stuck." I laugh so hard and she tries to hit me but I'm just out of her reach. I stand and stick my hand out to help her up. "Come on old lady." She pulls on my hand to stand.

"Don't make fun of me. When you are this old, I will haunt you. Push your ass down and laugh when you can't move." She looks serious but I know she isn't actually offended.

"Okay Ms. Beth, I'm sorry. I'll see you around. Don't sit on the ground anymore." I go back to my bike and swing my leg over and sit.

"Fuck off." Ms. Beth is the sweetest. I slide my helmet on and music is still playing. Shit, I forgot to turn it off. It's fine, all of the songs on here are good. I push back the kickstand and start my bike. It comes to life, I switch gears and drive off. *Cause day'n'nite the lonely stoner seems to free his mind at night.* This song just hits differently.

I lose track of time but when I see the ocean, I know it has been a little over an hour. I pull off to the side of the road and cut the engine, take my helmet off, and look out to the water. It's beautiful. The sky is full of pinks and oranges as the sun sets.

Today has been so shitty and this view makes it seem so irrelevant now. I pull my phone out and take a picture because I have to show this to the girls. I take my phone off do not disturb and send it in the group message. A few minutes later a notification pops up saying that I missed a call from the hospital.

I immediately call back and go through three different people before I get to the doctor that was taking care of Elise.

"Hello, what happened to Elise? Is she okay?"

"This is Doctor Sullivan and I was responsible for the care of Elise Warring. I'm sorry to say but Elise died fifteen minutes ago."

I take the phone away from my ear and look up to the sky and feel the tears welling up in my eyes. I give myself just a minute and then bring the phone back to my ear.

"I don't understand. I was told that the bullet was removed and she was okay."

"The bullet hit the rib and a fragment of the bone punctured her heart. We didn't see it when she was in surgery."

"Shit. Okay, thank you for calling me."

I hang up because I don't need him to tell me to come to the hospital to do any paperwork or anything. They will find out sooner or later that I'm not actually kin to her. I can't believe I killed her. How am I supposed to sleep at night?

I guess I can think about how Melody and Hasley are safe now. Yes, think about them. Neither of them texted me back so hopefully, they are asleep. I look back at the sunset which is almost completely gone.

I love them.

If they choose me, I will make them mine. I will have to do something to show my commitment to them. An idea pops into my head and I zip my phone back up in my jacket, put my helmet on, and start my bike. I'm so excited right now that I speed off with this stupid ass smile on my face.

I walk into my apartment and it's dark with only the stove light on. I lay my helmet, jacket, and keys on the couch. I slide my boots off and walk through the hallway to my room. The girls are spooning.

Melody is the big spoon and Hasley is the little one. I put the gift bag on the floor beside my room door, strip down, undo my hair, and snuggle up under the blankets with them. Melody's eyes pop open and I shush her. She smiles and goes back to sleep.

It doesn't take long and I'm right behind her.

Chapter 11

I wake to Melody kissing my shoulder.

"Good morning, pet. How are you feeling?" I ask her while I pull her up to steal a kiss on her lips. She hums in approval.

"Good actually. Hasley really took care of me last night while you were out galavanting," she quips but still smiling so I know it's just a joke.

"I'm sorry, I didn't mean to stay out so late. How about we wake Hasley up and start our day?" I ask but it's not an actual question. Melody walks around the bed and lightly pinches Hasley's nipples. I slide between Hasley's legs and nibble on her thighs. She starts to squirm but is still not awake.

I lick her pussy through her panties and a moan leaves her lips. Her hand goes to my head and she grinds against my face. I slide the thin cloth to the side and my tongue dives into her entrance. Her legs are tightening against my ears.

I lick up to her clit and suck while I push two fingers into her wet heat. I look up to see Melody sucking one nipple and pinching the other between her fingers. I look a little harder and notice Hasley has her hand playing with Melody's pussy. Fuck, this is so hot. Hasley's legs started shaking and Melody starts moaning with her.

"Fuck. Cum with me Melody," Hasley moans out and that takes me off guard because she does not dirty talk. They are both moaning loud now and I can feel Hasley shutter. With Melody's breathy noises, I know she is also cumming. It's like music and it's beautiful. After they come down from their orgasms, I tell them that we need to have a serious conversation.

"I need to know where y'all stand with me and what y'all are wanting out of this," I tell them both and hold my breath for an answer.

Hasley speaks up first. "I love you both and I don't want this to end. I know this started off as fun or maybe even a challenge to see if you can get the straight girl to turn gay, but I want to keep it going."

"When I took that pill and called you, I thought that was going to be the last time I would hear your voice. I thought that you wouldn't want me because I wasn't strong enough to keep clean and then everything that Elise told me, she made me sure of it. I love y'all and I want this forever. I don't know what I would do if this didn't work out. Y'all make me so happy." Melody starts crying while she gives me and Hasley her heart.

"I love you both too, so fucking much. I bought something. Neither of you has to accept it if it's moving too fast." I swear they can hear the nerves in my voice. I get up to get the little brown bag and hop back onto the bed. I pull out three little black boxes and give them the boxes with their initials. They wait for me and I tell them that they can open it and they pull the lid off. Their eyes light up and I see tears in Hasley's eyes. I gave them the same necklace—silver chain with a circle in the middle.

"I love it. Will you put it on me?" Hasley asks me and I slide over to help her. I kiss the back of her head and then look up to see Melody's reaction. She is staring at me with a smile and I notice that she put hers on already. I crawl over to her and give her a slow kiss but then pull away to show them what I got myself.

"I was going to get y'all actual collars but decided to go with something a little more discreet. I got myself one too but it's a little different," I tell them as I open my box and put my necklace on. It's a silver chain with two interlocking circles. "I got these for us to show our commitment. We obviously can't get married but I was hoping that this would be good enough."

"So is this like a proposal? I mean, yes, but I want to make sure before I get too excited," Melody asks me and I nod. They both jump on me at the same time and we spend the next two hours biting, sucking, licking, and so much cumming.

"Y'all are so cute together! Ahh, I love it. You look so amazing, Izzy. I like seeing you look like this." Clara tells me as she takes my money for mine and the girl's coffee.

"How do I look?" I ask utterly confused.

"Happy," Clara responds simply. I just smile at her and walk to the counter to wait on our drinks. Ash sets down the coffee and stares at me.

"What?" I ask her plainly.

"You better not miss my last dress fitting." Ash is so serious sometimes and it's cute.

"I'm not but why are you having one a few days before your wedding? If it doesn't fit then you're screwed either way." I instantly regret my words.

"Go fuck yourself. I hope when you walk outside, you step in a deep puddle." She gives me an eat-shit look. I just take the cups and slowly walk away. She's fucking crazy. I sit down at the table and give Hasley her caramel frappe and give Melody her black with a splash of half and half.

"I have to go to Ash's dress fitting later today. What are y'all going to be up to?" I ask them as I sip my mocha.

"I'm actually going to go to work and help the staff out. I've been a terrible owner lately." Hasley says.

"You have a manager there, right? As an owner, you shouldn't be there constantly." I tell her.

"Eh, I like being involved in my business. What about you? When's the last time you went to work?" Hasley calls me out.

"With everything that has happened, Jace told them that I needed a few personal days." I nod at her matter of factly.

"Y'all are funny. I'm about to go in. This guy has been wanting something on his ribs for the past week but I kept putting it off. I don't have a reason not to now." Melody pipes up.

"Oh, I have something I want to do tomorrow before Melody has to go to work," Hasley says and I just sit there and wait. She doesn't add anything to that.

"Am I supposed to guess or are you going to tell me?" I ask her.

"It's a surprise but I need you to take your bike to this place. I'll text you the address." That doesn't help me at all. I'm not a fan of surprises but I trust her. It just better not be something with an audience.

"Anyways, how do y'all feel about moving in with me?" I don't think it's out of the way to ask, I mean they are always there anyways.

"So you haven't noticed but I've been slowly moving in for about a week now. I bring small stuff in at a time." Melody says and I can't hide the shock on my face.

"Yeah, we kind of both have. At first, it was just the toiletries because I've been taking all of my showers while I'm there. But then I started bringing my vinyl player and clothes. I really only have furniture and artwork at my place." Hasley looks sheepish after admitting that.

"Well fuck me then." I am shocked and speechless.

"We had no plans to go anywhere. You were already stuck with us before you even decided on it," Melody says and takes a sip of her coffee.

"Y'all are fucking crazy," I shake my head with a straight face but they both laugh anyways.

"Yes, mommy, be afraid. I'm heading out. I love y'all." Melody kisses Hasley and then me on the lips. I notice the looks that the other coffee-getters are giving us but I ignore them. Well, I did ignore them until Hasley started to look uncomfortable. I stand up and look over at the people in the shop.

"I'm sorry, does anybody have a problem?" I wait for somebody to speak up but nobody has the balls to. "No? Okay then focus on choking on your drinks instead of what me and my wives are doing." I sit down and look up at Hasley. "What?"

"Did you just call us your wives?" She asks, her jaw dropping and I swear it hits the floor.

"Is that a problem?" I ask her.

"You can call me whatever you want." She says and leans over to kiss me. As we lock lips, I stick my middle finger up at anybody who's watching.

"Alright, go to work and I'll see you later tonight. I love you." I say and walk her to her car. I kiss her again before I open her door and watch her get buckled in. She blows me a kiss and I reach my hand up as I catch it. I never thought I would be that girl, you know, the one that makes people want to puke. But here I am, catching fucking air kisses. *What the fuck happened to me?*

I walk over to my bike and hop on, put my helmet on, push the kickstand back, and start her up. I drive to the bridal shop a little early to put my dress on. Traffic is decent today so getting there was quick and easy. When I park and walk in, I'm stopped but the same lady I met the first time. The one that had a stick up her ass. From the look she is giving me, it's still there.

"Welcome, how can I help you today?" She asks in a snarky tone.

"I was here before, I need to try on my dress for Ash's wedding this week," I tell her.

"This week? Cutting it a little close." Fuck this lady.

"Just because you aren't getting fucked the right way doesn't mean you need to be snarky." I snap. I head to the little section at the back where there are two chairs, a couch, and a small stage with mirrors. The lady disappears but then reappears with an aqua dress. She hands it to me and it's a beautiful silk. I take it to the dressing room to put it on and when I'm back in front of the mirror, I'm gaping. It's a halter with a deep v-cut in the front.

There's a ribbon sash that crosses my back, wraps around my midsection, and ties in the back. Right above my ass. Okay but the way this dress makes my tits look is insane. Ash has damn good taste. I thought she was going to put me in a God-awful thing.

"Oh. My. God! Izzy, you look beautiful." Ash screams from behind me. I turn to look at her and of course, she's crying again.

"You have got to get yourself in check. You can't cry every five seconds." I whisper but still loud enough to where she could hear me.

"Fine, hurry up and change so I can put mine on." She orders and I do as I'm told.

When I'm back in my leathers, I sit in one of the chairs and watch Ash walk out in this amazing white dress. It looks like a boho kind of dress. It's a v-cut front with thin straps, an open back, a thick glitter belt right under the breast, and a loose wavy bottom. "What do you think? Does it hide my bump?"

"You're beautiful, Ash. And yes, it hides the baby pooch." I say with a wink. She hates when I call it that. The sales lady walks up to me again.

"Would you like some champagne?" She asks me.

"No, but thank you," I tell her in my nicest voice. Ash looks at me like I'm growing another head.

"When have you ever passed up on alcohol?" Ash asks me.

"The girls and I are dealing with a problem and I want to be supportive. So, I don't drink anymore," I tell her very nonchalantly.

"That's very sweet of you. How's Melody doing?" She asks as she walks back to the dressing room to change back into her clothes. I follow but stay on the other side of the door.

"She is acting fine and she says she's fine," I tell her through the door.

"But you don't think she is?" Ash is bright and doesn't ever hold back her concerns.

"I mean, a lot has happened to her. Some things that I don't know if she is ready to tell anybody. But even with just being taken, that's hard on her. We haven't sat down and talked but I know we need to. Or at least she needs to talk to somebody. Ya, know?" At this point, I feel like I'm just venting.

"Ahh! Can you please come help me take this damn thing off?" She yells out in frustration. I walk in and the sight in front of me almost has me falling over with laughter. This girl is laying on her side, trying to reach the zipper on the back of the dress. "If I wasn't on this floor,

I would punch you. Now if you can contain yourself for a minute and help me, that would be fucking amazing."

"Okay but hang on, I have to take a picture." I pull my phone out and snap a couple of photos. She gives me a 'fuck you' look but I don't care, this is fucking hilarious. After I got a few, I put my phone back in my pocket and help her stand up. She steps on the dress and curses, I'm dying. I help her stand and unzip the dress, take her hand, and help her step out of it. She's wearing this sexy matching black lace bra and panties. When my eyes make it up to hers, she has a knowing look.

"Keep it up and Jace might get a little jealous." She says and smirks. I just shake my head and hang the dress on the black, velvet hanger.

When Ash has her clothes on, I take the dress and open the dressing room door. She steps in front of me and I follow her lead, all the way to her car. She opens the back seat door and I hang the dress on the car hook. I give her a hug and we say our goodbyes.

Chapter 12

"Okay, Hasley, straddle the bike but bend over so that you're laying down... Perfect, just like that. Maybe cross your arms under your head. Yes! Now Izzy, stand behind her and grab her ass with both hands... There you go. Look down at her ass like you want to bite it. Melody, come over to this side of the bike and get on your knees. Right there under Hasley's face. Beautiful." The photographer says.

I'm wearing a black corset with a lace garter belt that hooks the black garters on each thigh and black lace panties. Hasley and Melody are only wearing black thongs. The sex after this is going to be so fucking good. With every squeeze of Hasley's ass, she lets out a quiet moan so I know she's soaked.

"Hasley, drop your right arm. Okay now cup Melody's cheek. Perfect. Melody, look up at Hasley a little more. Y'all look so damn hot." The photographer praises us as she takes the pictures. She changes our positions a few times and this is actually turning out to be fun. The girls are pretty fucking sexy.

The last position that we are put in is too tempting to pass up. I'm straddling my bike, Melody is straddling me. She's leaning back with her hands holding onto the handlebars. Her back is arched, her breasts pushed up, and is almost in my face. Hasley is standing on my left side and her hand is on Melody's neck.

I hear the clicks of the camera but I also feel the heat of Melody's pussy on my lap. I look over at the photographer and wink. She's about to get a whole lot of sexy. I push Melody's panties to the side just enough to plunge my middle finger into her. Her mouth opens wide and her eyes screw shut.

I zone out the photographer and focus on my girl. She feels so good around my finger. While I pump my finger in her, my thumb circles her clit. I lick up her chest and stop at the swell of her breast. I suck my way up to her nipple and my mouth clamps around it.

Her body jerks and she moans. Hasley darts her tongue in Melody's open mouth, her hand still around her neck. When Melody's legs start to shake, I push another finger into her and her pussy clenches around my fingers. Hasley has put a little pressure on Melody's neck and I think Melody is into that.

Oh, the things that I could do with that information.

When Melody comes back down to me, I pull my fingers out of her and make Hasley lick them clean. I hear the clicking of the camera and I pull my brain back to where we are right now.

"Well, ladies. I got quite a few steamy shots. I'm going to take this to my office and make some edits. I'll email them to you when I finish. Is there anything else you need?" The photographer asks. I don't even look her way. I keep my eyes on the sexiness in front of me.

"Yeah, I need you to leave so that I can properly fuck what's mine," I say with a growl.

"But you're in public…" she says.

"Leave," I demand and kiss Melody, hard. Yes, we are in the middle of the woods and I guess somebody could walk up but that probably won't happen. I don't wait for the photographer to walk away before I get off of the bike, tell Melody to get up, and make Hasley lay on it.

"Just like the way Melody was. And Melody, bend over the back." I order and they follow without question. I sink to my knees behind Melody and lick up her thighs, slowly. I know it's torture when she shakes her ass for me to hurry.

"Are you rushing me, pet?" I love when we play and we are in a scene.

"No, mommy. I'm sorry." Melody apologizes. I slap her ass one good time and she tries to hide the scream. It sounds muffled so she must have already started eating Hasley. I wanted to string this out longer but I want to taste her too bad for that. I dive into her pussy and she moans.

They are so loud it wouldn't surprise me if somebody did hear them. My knees hurt from the sticks and leaves but I focus on getting Melody to the high that she needs. Hasley's moans start to become a high pitch which tells me that she is cumming. Not long after her, Melody is cumming on my tongue.

I give them a minute to compose themselves and then I help them get dressed. I put my pants on and my leather jacket, walk them to Halsey's car and I walk back to get on my motorcycle and head home.

The day before the wedding is ridiculous. The wedding planner is yelling at everybody and Silas is sneaking beer. This was supposed to be a quick rehearsal but here we are, an hour in, and haven't even started. Ms. Beth let Ash and Jace have their wedding at her barn behind her house.

Ash said it's going to be a small get-together because neither of them like people. *Wait, what did she say... oh yeah, she said it was 'too peopley'.* I'm about to get my girls and leave. Melody is fidgeting and scratching her arm. She's wanting something to buzz on. I don't like her feeling this way.

"Hold onto Melody, I'm going to try to hurry this along," I whisper to Hasley. Melody doesn't need to know that she is being kept. I walk around looking for Jace because there is no way in hell I'm talking to Ash about this. Her hormones are too much for me. *Yeah, fuck that.* It takes a minute but I finally find him... well, hear him.

"Fuck, Ash. Just like that." Jace moans.

"OMG! You're so deep like this. Fuck me faster, Jace." Ash yells out.

Okay then. That's my cue to leave. Good for him but I'm not going to stick around any longer. I know what to do, walk down the aisle and stand there. Nothing crazy.

I get back to Hasley and Melody and tell them that it's time to go.

"Wait, nothing happened," Melody says.

"At the moment Ash is wetting Jace's dick, we aren't missing out on anything. So, let's go," I say and tug them along to my car.

"Since we are leaving early, can you drop me off at the church down the road? They are having an NA meeting and I think I need to go." Melody says with tears in her eyes.

"We will wait for you in the parking lot," I tell her and take her in my arms for a hug. Hasley throws her arms around us too. We all break out laughing and get in the car.

"How did your meeting go?" I ask Melody when she gets in the passenger seat. She has tears streaming down her face and I don't like it.

"I'm sorry, I don't mean to be so upset. I got my one-day chip and it's killing me." She hiccups.

"Melody, it's nothing to be ashamed of. You noticed that you needed help and you reached out to get it. You shouldn't feel the best but definitely not so upset. I'm proud of you," I try to talk her up and maybe get her to slow down on the crying.

"You don't understand! I had five years! Five years, Izzy! This stupid one-day coin is nothing compared to the one that says five years." She has snot coming out of her nose, mixing with the tears from her eyes. I pull her to me and hug her for a few minutes.

"Melody, I am so fucking proud of you. Yeah, it's not five years anymore but you know what? You decided that being clean means a lot and it's worth starting over instead of giving in and giving up. I will help you through this." I pull away from her and clasp Hasley's hand. "We will help you through this." She slowly stops crying and I wipe her face with a tissue. When she is breathing calmly again, I ask her if I could see the coin. It's gold with the number 1 on one side and a prayer on the other that says 'GOD GRANT ME THE SERENITY TO ACCEPT THE THINGS THAT I CANNOT CHANGE, COURAGE TO CHANGE THE THINGS I CAN, AND WISDOM TO KNOW THE DIFFERENCE'.

"This is beautiful and I'm looking forward to seeing the next one that you get," I tell her and drive us home. Since they were already slowly moving in before, it didn't take much to get them fully in here. I did have to buy a new bed. I put two kings together and made one huge bed that takes up most of our room.

"I think we need a bath. What do you think, mommy?" Hasley asks and bites her bottom lip. I look over to Melody and she's smiling the sexiest smile I've ever seen.

"I'll start it, go get ready." I tilt my head to the bedroom and I go to the bathroom, starting the bath water. I pour some bubbles in and swoosh it around with my hands. They come in as I stand up but I'm not ready yet. The water needs to get higher and I need to get some bottles of water to drink. When I come back to the bathroom with the bottles, the girls are already in and started making out.

"Hey! I never said to get in." I raise my voice to them. We are in a scene and they are doing things before the permission was given. "Get out. Now." They hurry out and Hasley almost slips and falls. I strip down and get in the bath, turn the water off, and enjoy the warmth while the girls are shivering. I sit on my knees, cup my breasts, and moan in enjoyment. I pinch my nipples and let my head fall back.

When I'm bored with that, I get up to sit on the edge of the tub. Spreading my legs, I give them a full view of me circling my clit. I slide two fingers in and pull them out to play with my clit again. A little bit of pressure and the look on their faces and I'm cumming.

When I can get words out, I tell them to come clean me up. They rush over and slide to their knees. Both of their tongues are licking my pussy. That sight alone has my legs shaking.

"Oh, fuck. Don't stop. Y'all look so fucking amazing. Just like that. Lick mommy's pussy like good fucking girls." I start to spasm and somebody pushes their fingers in me. I cum so hard in their mouths. "Fuuck, yes!" I squeak. When I finish, I get back into the bath.

"Which one of you can hold your breath for a long time?" I ask them because there's something that I want to try.

"I want to play," Melody speaks up. I wrap my hand around her neck and slowly push her down, right before she goes under I tell her the rules.

"When you are getting uncomfortable, tap my arm once. When you have had enough, tap my arm twice." She nods.

"I need words, Melody." I scold her. This is about trust and I need to know that she fully gets what's happening.

"Tap once if I get close and two times when I need air." She confirms. With that, push her under and keep my hand on her neck. I play with her nipples and slide my hand down her body to cup her heat. Air bubbles float to the surface but she hasn't tapped out yet.

"Hasley, is this hot?" I don't want her to be left out.

"Yes, mommy." She says, breathy.

"Does this make you wet?" I ask

"Yes, mommy." She says again.

"Touch yourself, pet," I command her, not taking my eyes off Melody. I shove a finger into her and more air bubbles meet the surface. I pick up speed and when I hear Hasley start cumming, I curve my finger into a hook and hit Melody's G-spot. She double taps my arm and I am immediately out of her and pull her up for air.

"No, don't stop." She says while trying to catch her breath. I push my finger back into her and find that sweet spot again. She is cumming within seconds and Hasley is swallowing Melody's moans. Fuck, this is the hottest thing I have ever seen.

After we actually bathe, we lay in bed and sleep the whole night.

· ♥ · ♥ · ♥ · ♥ · ♥ ·

"Places! Places, everybody!" The wedding planner practically screams. I try to hold back a laugh but honestly, her face is just too funny. I swear I can see the veins pop out of her neck and forehead. Jace is already at the altar but I know he would be cracking up right here with me if he could. I take Silas's arm and we walk toward the preacher.

"You look really pretty, Izzy." Silas looks up and says.

"Shut up little kid," I tell him but the smile I give him shows that I'm just playing around. When we make it up to Jace, I let go of Silas and take my position on the opposite side. When Ash asked me to be her maid of honor, I was really surprised but of course, I said *hell yes*. After the other bridesmaids walk down the aisle with the groomsmen, the wedding song begins and Ash is next.

She's beautiful.

I notice nobody walking with her and her eyes wandering, I take the risk and meet her halfway. I stick my elbow out and she grabs onto it, walking the rest of the way. When we make it to Jace, I kiss her cheek and take my place back with the other ladies. Ash looks back to tell me 'thank you' but I wave her off.

She looks down, bringing my eyes with hers. She sticks her foot out of her dress and just like her, she's wearing those fucking Vans. Why did I think she was going to be normal and wear heels? I laugh to myself and shake my head.

The rest of the service was more funny than sweet. It only made sense with them. The reception, on the other hand, was a little wild. So many people were drunk before we even got to the cake-cutting. I kept my hand in Melody's the whole time.

"Why don't you have a drink?" Melody asks me like she doesn't already know.

"I don't want one. We already talked about how I don't do that anymore," I tell her.

"It's okay, really." Melody tries again. I pull her outside of Ms. Beth's barn and slam her against a tree.

"Do not question me again. I told you that I am in this with you, the whole fucking way. The good and the bad. I don't know what kind of dipshit you were with before, but I respect you and what you are going through. Do you understand me?" I say between clenched teeth. She wraps her hands around the back of my neck and pulls me in for a rough, sloppy, needy kiss. "Fuck, I want to dip my fingers in you right here," I confess. She's wearing a black miniskirt so all she needs to do is give me the green light.

"When have you ever held back?" She says and that's it for me. I look around really fast and I know I won't see anybody because Jace and Ash are cutting their 4-tier cake. I put my fingers in her face and tell her to suck. She makes a show of it but we don't have time for all of that.

I pull my fingers out with a pop, hold her right thigh up to my waist, and plunge my two fingers inside her. Her head falls back and hits the tree but she likes the pain. I'm pumping into her fast and she's already so close. I feel her pussy tighten and she's about to go over.

"That's right. Cum for me, pet. I want your cum dripping down my hand." I encourage her. Once she starts to make a little noise, I throw my lips on hers in a hungry kiss. When she comes down from the orgasm, I drop her leg and hold her until she can stand on her own.

"I needed that, thank you." She says.

"You know what, I like that. I might make y'all thank me every time I allow y'all to cum. She smiles but doesn't dare roll her eyes. When we turn around, Ash is standing there.

"Now that you have finished, can we gather to do the bouquet toss? Or would you like me to make everybody leave so that y'all can fuck on the table?" Ash asks, jokingly.

"You would do that for me? Thank you so much." I say back. She just smiles and shakes her head.

"Let's go, horndogs." She takes the lead and we follow with the biggest smiles on our faces.

Clara catches the bouquet and her cheeks turn a strawberry red. It's adorable.

"Now that all this wedding stuff is over, how about we take that trip I promised?" I ask Melody and Hasley.

"That sounds perfect," Melody says first.

"I can't wait to be alone with y'all," Hasley squeals and bites her bottom lip.

Acknowledgments

S.L. Forrester-

I would like to thank all of you for reading Yes Ma'am.

Kate, it has been so much fun writing with you. You are so sweet and such a good friend!

Ashley, you have been so supportive and helping every step of the way, again. I'm so lucky to have y'all and there will be no running away!

Also, Carmen, you did it again! The cover is freaking amazing and the chapter pages are everything I wanted.

Thank you to my amazing beta readers, Carol-Ann and Vanessa!

Arc readers, y'all are superstars and I am so lucky that I have you.

I want to thank my three kids for their support. Y'all are my rock, even though this book will never touch your innocent hands.

Kate-Lynn Elizabeth-

I don't think I will get used to writing this part of the book, probably ever. There are way too many people to thank and acknowledge through the process of writing a book, and I don't want to leave anyone out by accident. So as a cursory, I'M SORRY! Too Canadian? Maybe this will help, to everyone who helped with this book THANK YOU! You are amazing and I love you. Thank you for following along with S.L.Forrester and I on this journey from when it was just a theory that was thrown out over a late night sprint conversation. Now let's get into the individual thank yous now that I have done my due diligence of thanking everyone first, eh? Now that's too Canadian!

Shelby - My co-author. My Friend. Someone I know I can go to with anything and you won't judge me for it. You are the FREAKING BEST! I LOVED writing this with you and I greatly appreciate you allowing me to tag along on this journey with you and Izzy's HEA. I cannot wait to see what we write together next!

MM - My partner. My love. Thank you so much for supporting me and loving me, even when I got crazy and decided to become an author and got super hyper fixated on starting my debut that still hasn't been released. Hopefully soon. I am so thankful for all the unbiased writing advice you have given on what to do with the storyline and always offering your services to take my mind off things when I get overwhelmed with everything. I love you!

Amy - My friend, author of the amazing Centaur tribe series. (If you love fantasy romance, read Amy Lee's Centaur tribe series on KU. Start with Fate and Resolve and sign up for her newsletter to get bonus material!) You have helped me soooo much on what certain things are good and bad in editing. My writing would be atrocious without your help. Thank you!

Aly - You and Amy (besides MM) are my ride or die girls! I can literally send some random line in our group chat and you are ALWAYS down to talk about whatever. Late night reads, chats, and picture sharing. I know if I get insomnia I can message you (since you are 3 hours in the past!) that you will most likely be awake for a bit. We need to keep reading that book! It's been forever!

Betas - Carol-Ann and Vanessa, you are an integral part of publishing a novel! Thank you so much for reading the story and making sure it made sense on the reader's side as we knew what was supposed to be going on and had to make sure that came across to the reader as well. I loved reading all your comments and thoughts along the way and I hope you stick with us and the series as it progresses!

ARC readers - Thank you so much for taking the time to read our little novel! I am blown away that so many people dedicate their time to reading and talking about a book before its release. It really helps us out as authors to get the book out there.

About Authors

S.L.Forrester is the author of Spice, Sass, and HEAs'. She lives in South Carolina with her husband and 3 kids. When she isn't writing, she's either dancing in her living room or reading. She listens to anything from country to 90s music and she reads fantasy and smut. Loads of smut. She cares for her friends like they are family.

If you want to follow her for future writings, look her up on Instagram, TikTok, Facebook, and Clapper at-
@S.L.Forrester

Kate-Lynn Elizabeth is an author of HEAs, but puts her characters through some issues to get there. Co-writing with the amazing S.L. Forrester is fabulous. She lives in the snowy north of Canada and spends her time mostly reading, cuddling with her beautiful black and white spoiled tuxedo cat, Bella, or rewatching some of her comfort shows on Disney+. She's watched *Criminal minds,* and *Bones* countless times and now uses them as background noise.

Also By S.L.Forrester

Taking The Shot

www.ingramcontent.com/pod-product-compliance
Lightning Source LLC
LaVergne TN
LVHW010322070526
838199LV00065B/5635